To Angie Van de water

Thank you for supporting my dream. I hope you enjoy the journey.

Life can be sweet without sugar!

Rodolfo
x Fernandes

HEALTHY, DELICIOUS & NUTRITIOUS FOODS YOU WILL LOVE TO EAT

YOU WILL

NEVER BE

HUNGRY

AGAIN

RODOLFO FERNANDES

Written and published by

Rodolfo Fernandes

www.neverhungryagain.com

Food Photography

Rodolfo Fernandes

Cover Photo

Carlos Carpio

Copy Editor

Luis Carpio, Consulting, F. P.

ISBN 978-1-5323-2511-3

Ebook ISBN 978-1-5323-2512-0

Printed in China

First Edition 2017

Rodolfo is a chef who started cooking at a very young age with his mother in Brazil and later went on to study Culinary Arts in Scotland, Mexico City and Houston. From his mother he acquired not just his love of cooking and preparing comfort food, but also the creativity to work with what was on hand. His Culinary journey led him to study hospitality in Aberdeen, which cemented his love of cooking, going on to perfect his craft in Le Cordon Bleu in Mexico, where he earned the highest Culinary and Pastry degrees, as well as one in Mexican cuisine. He later topped his skills with a degree in Culinary Management at the Culinary Institute Lenôtre in Houston.

These culinary skills and creativity, as well as the industry management know-how, have allowed him to explore new and healthier ways to prepare comfort food in a style he calls "well-prepared food"; a new, simpler style that does not sacrifice content and flavor by using technique to create healthier options that you will be as happy to eat as those prepared more elaborately.

This book is for people who;

- Enjoy food, flavors and the experience of eating.

- Are not professional or frequent cooks but would still like to prepare their own meals.

- Want to eat better without sacrificing flavor or the experience of eating good food.

- Are eternally on a strict diet but gain all the weight back (and more) the moment they stop depriving themselves of food.

- Need to control fat, sugar, or salt due to their health or lifestyle choice.

- Eat mostly healthy during the work-week, but find they cannot control what they eat at night or over the weekend.

- Want to learn how to prepare flavorful, quick, and easy to prepare, affordable meals.

- Have someone in their family who needs to eat healthy but are trapped in the takeout and junk-food

  culture.

In This Book, I will show you how to prepare affordable, simple, quick, nutritious and delicious foods, making 5 star meals with easy to source ingredients and most important, while staying and feeling healthier.

1,2,3...

Using step-by-step guided instructions, this book demonstrates that it is possible to eat healthy and satisfyingly and still lose weight. This is a life-style-changing book that only asks you to venture into cooking some very flavorful dishes and to realize that a healthy burger with "french fries" can be as healthy as a salad. Better still, it will not leave you hungry while ensuring that you get all the nutrients (proteins, fat and carbs) required for a healthy body, and taking you off the dieting rollercoaster.

Common reasons people stop cooking.

1. I can't cook.

2. I don't have time to cook.

3. Is too difficult and I don't understand cooking terms.

4. Kitchen tools are too complicated.

5. I hate cleaning afterward.

6. I hate cooking just for myself.

These are the most common reasons I hear when I ask my clients why they are not cooking their own meals. Before writing this book I spent countless hours reading cookbook reviews and complaints, taking note of everything that could possibly keep someone from cooking. My goal with this book is to show you that cooking can be simple and enjoyable.

Anyone can cook, yes anyone. As a chef de cuisine/pastry chef I took it upon myself to identify why some people can't or won't cook and the most common reasons I found where that; a) they do not follow recipes correctly, b) their recipes were not tested by authors, c) they have problems with the quantity of seasonings or d) complicated cooking terms were used to explain simple things.

They say cooking is an art and pastry is a science, the reason being that cooking is usually about "a pinch of this", "season to taste" and "substitutions", as well as many "etc." and variables, so it can be hit or miss if you are not experienced. Pastry cooking, on the other hand, is exact. In pastry cooking, if you do not use the exact number and amount of ingredients (all) in the exact measure it simply will not work. This previous statement may strike fear into some, but if you look at it on the bright side, it can actually be a blessing for the novice cook. For this book I applied pastry techniques to cooking, meaning that if you measure everything exactly as given and add some loving care, all your meals will be perfect and you will be amazed how easy is to put a nice dish on the table.

Find time. If you go back 10-15 years and asked someone about cooking their own meals, the excuse would almost always be the same "I don't have time". Now think of the present; years ago we didn't have as much social media in our life as we have today yet we still find an amazing amount of time for it. If you have 2-3 hours to spend on social media, you will have 30 minutes to cook your own food. Just think about it; this is your body and the time for a change is NOW. Cooking your own meals is the most effective way to be healthy and lose and/or maintain weight. Even before becoming a Chef, I used to cook for everyone but was too lazy to cook my own meals. The best and easiest option was to eat out, buy precooked, ready-to-eat meals or just opt for take-out junk food. The problem with that approach is that none of those "options" improve the nutrients going into your body or benefit your health.

The main concern and common theme in all these solutions is how to achieve taste (high sodium, high in sugar, artificial flavors, chemicals etc.) with the lowest amount of expensive nutrients (like protein, quality fats and carbs). As a result of my approach to feeding myself I ended up cooking healthy food for my clients while living an unhealthy life myself. At the peak of my bad health I was hypertensive, with a high body fat index. Even though I spent countless hours at the gym each week, I looked big but not in a healthy way, which should be the goal.(1)

It can be easy. That is the main reason why I wanted to create a cookbook with step by step photos and **no** complicated cooking terminology or methods. Everything here is as simple as it could possibly be. I used affordable ingredients that may be found at any mayor supermarket and are common for many uses. If you look trough the recipes you will see that the ingredients are pretty much the same, meaning that you can create different recipes using the same ingredients in your pantry.

Can you turn on a blender, stove or a microwave? If you can, then you are all set; most recipes are microwave-friendly, requiring no complicated food processor. Usually, a regular pot or pan will be enough to prepare the meals. I am not preaching against specialized and sophisticated kitchen utensils, they are great! If you have them, want them, like them and know how to use them "more power to you" but not having them is not and excuse for not cooking.

I also hate cleaning, and therefore did not include the use of food processors or any other kitchen tool that will be a nightmare to clean after use.

(1) If you want to know more about my journey with food and how I went from unhealthy because of food and then healthy with food as my savior go to www.neverhungryagain.com.

To reduce the time spent cleaning after cooking, most of my recipes are one-pot; complete meals that are easy to plate and clean afterwards. My method for each and every recipe in this book was "clean-as-you-go", meaning that, in 30 minutes or so, you will be all set to enjoy your meal without all the aftermath. This is especially useful when cooking for your partner or friends and you don't want to be in the kitchen cleaning for hours after you have finished the meal.

Cooking for one? As you may imagine, even for a chef, cooking for one person is as much of a nuisance as is dealing with leftovers. Here again, a negative can be a positive, these recipes are not only scalable but most of them can be divided into portions that will keep for up to 4-5 days with proper refrigeration. As complete meals so you can divide the portions and refrigerate for up to 4-5 days. For more flexibility, you can freeze the portioned meals for up to 4-5 months. That way you can always have something available for an even quicker meal by taking out something *you made* from the refrigerator or freezer and popping it in the microwave.(2)

Another option is to find a friend or family-member with the same desire for a change and cook for each other on alternate days. Motivation is the key for a successful healthy life-style. Be creative. Find ways that will make you keep going and changing your bad eating-habits and I can guarantee that you will feel AMAZING.

 (2) Refrigeration is done in a normal refrigerator between 34 and 40 °F (1-4 C°) and Freezing is done in the freezer where temperature is at 0°F (-18°C) or lower. Buy freezer proof containers with lids, put label with the description of the food and the date so you can later identify and track them (it's amazingly easy to forget what something "is" or "when" you froze it).

6 Reasons to not eat out

- Cooking gives you a chance to be creative.

- You will be 100% in charge of what goes inside your body.

- You can be free from the temptation of eating high-calorie meals and large portions.

- Eating out is more expensive than eating in.

- Enjoy more time eating with your family. Cooking and eating together is the most precious experience a   family can have.

- The only effective way to lose or keep a healthy weight is to know exactly what you are eating, and when it is prepared by you the results are guaranteed.

After reading all of this, are you ready to take this journey with me and start cooking? Yes?! lets Cook!

BASIC COOKING TERMS

Al dente- An Italian term for cooked pasta that is cooked but still slightly firm not soggy or overcooked.

Bake -To cook something in an oven.

Beat -To mix ingredients together using a fast, circular movement it can be done by using a spoon, fork, whisk or mixer.

Blend -To mix ingredients together until well combined.

Brush - To coat food using a brush.

Boil -To heat a food/water so that the liquid gets hot enough until bubbles form and start to break continually on the surface.

Brown -To cook over medium or high heat until surface of food browns or darkens.

Chop -To cut into small pieces.

Dice -To cut into small cubes.

Drizzle - to pour olive oil or any liquid in a fine stream.

Drain -To remove all the liquid using a colander or a strainer.

Garnish - To decorate a food usually with another colorful food.

Grate or Shred -To scrape food against the holes of a grater making bits or shreds.

Grease -To lightly coats a surface so food does not stick when cooking or baking.

Knead -To stretch, press or fold dough until it is smooth and uniform, normally done by hands.

Mash -To squash food with a fork, spoon, or masher.

Mince -To cut into very small pieces, smaller than chopped or diced pieces .

Mix -To stir ingredients together until well combined.

Preheat -To turn oven/pan on ahead of time so that it is at the desired temperature when needed.

Purée- To mash or blend foods until smooth.

Peel- To remove skin from food or vegetables.

Season - To add salt, pepper, spices to enhance food flavor.

Simmer -To cook in liquid over low heat.

Stir Fry -To quickly cook food over high heat while constantly stirring the food.

Salt and pepper To taste- To add salt and pepper according to your personal preference, start by adding a pinch then mix and taste. If feel that it needs more, add a little more until you are satisfied with the taste. (Always being careful if your diet is a low in sodium diet)

Toss - To combine or mix ingredients with a lifting motion until well combined.

Reading food labels is sometimes tricky and it can be confusing, not just because understanding the information requires knowing precisely what you are looking for, but the lack of some standards on how to report does leave a great space for food companies to "play" creatively when supplying information (i.e. play with quantities, portions etc. so make it look like it is not as bad as it is). Here are some basic thing to look for and as the title suggest this is not intended as a deep dive into the subject but to provide some easy to learn tips and open you up for investigating further if you have a particular area that may be of mayor interest to you for personal/medical reasons.

Nutrition Facts

Serving Size 1 pack (38g)
Servings Per Container 9

Amount Per Serving	
Calories 190	Calories from fat 80

	%Daily Value
Total Fat 9g	14%
Saturated Fat 3.5	18%
Trans Fat 0g	
Cholesterol Less than 5mg	1%
Sodium 320mg	13%
Total Carbohydrate 23g	8%
Dietary Fiber 2g	8%
Sugar 4g	
Protein 3g	

Vitamin A 0%	-	Vitamin C 0%	
Calcium 8%	-	Iron 6%	

*Percent Daily Value are based on a 2,000 calories diet. Your daily values may be higher or lower depending on your needs:

FOOD LABELS 101

Start by checking serving size and serving per container as many times this is where the tricky part is. Sometimes you read a label and the calories amount looks great but, remember to always check the serving size, if it is too small then the information may be misleading. A label saying 5 Calories per serving may sound good until you find out its per gram, then it becomes a whole different number if the amount you plan to use is 100g. See how easy 5 Calories turn to 500 when you multiply!

Too much cholesterol can increase the risk of heart disease and other illnesses. Try to limit these to a recommended value. The amount recommended for a person with a 2000 calorie diet is no more than 300mg daily

Too much sodium is also not good for your health and can lead to serious health issues, mainly high blood pressure. The daily recommended amount is less than 2,400mg about 1 teaspoon. Ask you GP doctor what is your daily recommended amount as it may vary from person to person and health profile to health profile.

Choosing the right ingredients also means that you must read and understand food labels.

Nutrition Facts

Serving Size 1 pack (38g)
Servings Per Container 9

Amount Per Serving

Calories 190   Calories from fat 80

	%Daily Value
Total Fat 9g	**14%**
Saturated Fat 3.5	**18%**
Trans Fat 0g	
Cholesterol Less than 5mg	**1%**
Sodium 320mg	**13%**
Total Carbohydrate 23g	**8%**
Dietary Fiber 2g	**8%**
Sugar 4g	
Protein 3g	
Vitamin A 0% - Vitamin C 0%	
Calcium 8% - Iron 6%	

*Percent Daily Value are based on a 2,000 calories diet. Your daily values may be higher or lower depending on your needs:

Footnote

These are the total values recommended for a diet based on 2000-25000 daily calories .

When dealing with Saturated Fat and Trans fat, try to see the percentage value more than the mgs, why ? because if the amount of trans fat is less than 0.5g manufactures do not have to list on the labels so may even appear as zero (0). Always try to limit Saturated fat and trans fat. A quick guide: if the percentage is less than 5% is considered low if it is more than 20% is considered high.

Look for food that it is low in sugar, less than 10g of sugar is a good number and of course again it will depend on your health profile so consulting your GP is always a good idea. Nonetheless, a general solid rule is that too much sugar, over time can progress to Type 2 diabetes and many other illnesses.

Not all proteins are created alike. Try to eat clean sources of protein so choose foods that are lower in saturated fat yet have a high protein yield. This of course is a basic rule that is true in most cases but has its exceptions in fatty fishes, nuts and seeds which although high in fats it is good fat because it is Omega 3.

RECIPES

KITCHEN TOOLS

THE LIST:

. STRAINER.

. GRATER.

. BLENDER.

. CHEF'S KNIFE.

. PAIRING KNIFE.

.VEGETABLE PEELER.

.TIMER.

.WHISK.

.WOODEN SPOON.

. TONG.

. PREP BOWLS.

. MIXING BOWLS.

. ROLLING PIN.

. NON-STICK FRYING PAN

. RUBBER SPATULA.

.SILVERWARE.

. MEASURING CUPS.

. MEASURING SPOONS.

. BAKING PANS.

. ROUND COOKIE CUTTER.

. KITCHEN SCISSORS.

. CAN OPENER.

.COLANDER.

I wanted to make this book as simple as possible, all the recipes were made using these basics kitchen tools.

SEASONING RECIPES

All-purpose Latin America

2 tablespoons, Kosher salt.
1 tablespoon, ground black pepper.
1 tablespoon, dry oregano.
½ tablespoon, turmeric.
½ teaspoon, paprika.
½ teaspoon, dry cilantro.
1 tablespoon, garlic powder.

Calories per ½ teaspoon 2, Sodium 320mg.

Seasoned salt (reduced sodium)

1 tablespoon, Kosher salt.
1 tablespoon, paprika.
1 tablespoon, turmeric.
1 tablespoon, cornstarch.
2 tablespoons, onion powder.
2 tablespoons, garlic powder.
1 tablespoon, dry cilantro.
Pinch, cayenne pepper.(⅛ teaspoon)
½ tablespoon, brown sugar.

Calories per ½ teaspoon 3, Sodium 97mg

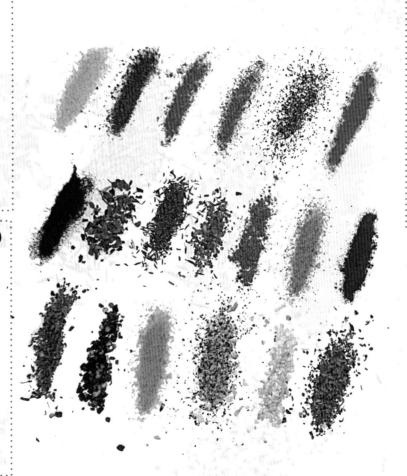

All-purpose salt free

1 tablespoon, onion powder.
1 tablespoon, dry oregano.
1 tablespoon, dry parsley.
1 tablespoon, dry thyme.
1 tablespoon, paprika.
1 tablespoon, garlic powder.
1 tablespoon, turmeric.
1 tablespoon, red pepper powder.

Calories per ½ teaspoon 1, Sodium 0.

All- purpose salt free (spicy)

1 tablespoon, chipotle powder.
1 tablespoon, smoked paprika.
1 tablespoon, onion powder.
1 tablespoon, garlic powder.
1 tablespoon, dry cilantro.
1 tablespoon, turmeric.
½ teaspoon, cayenne pepper.
1 tablespoon, dry oregano.

Calories per ½ teaspoon 1, Sodium 0.

Directions: Add all spices into a container with lid and give a good shake until all ingredients are mixed together. If you want a finer texture you can blend it to break down the pieces or use a spice grinder. Store in a small spice jar or, mason jar with a lid.

Lets cook!

MEAT

EGGPLANT LASAGNA

Total time: 50 min.

Prep: 25 min.

Cook: 25 min.

Yield: 8 servings.

Ingredients:

2 lbs. (907 g) 90% lean ground beef.

2 large eggplants, sliced ½ (1.27cm) inch thick.

1 large yellow onion, chopped.

½ cup green onions, chopped.

½ cup Italian parsley, chopped.

1 large can natural tomato sauce.

2 teaspoons reduced-sodium seasoned salt.

15 slices reduced fat turkey ham.

For the white sauce:

2 cups fat-free plain Greek yogurt.

1 cup low-fat mozzarella cheese.

1 large egg.

2 tablespoons green onion, chopped.

2 tablespoons Italian parsley, chopped.

Salt and pepper to taste.

1. Preheat oven to 425 °F (218 °C). Lightly grease a 13"x9" (33 x 23 cm) baking-dish with cooking-spray and set aside.

2. Place ground beef in a large, nonstick frying pan over medium-high heat. Crumble the meat in small pieces with wood or plastic utensil while cooking to facilitate cooking and prevent clumps. Cook for about 5 minutes. There is no need to add any fat.

4. In the same frying pan, over medium-high heat, cook chopped onions until translucent, (about 3 minutes) add the meat, tomato sauce, seasoned salt and chopped parsley. Mix well. You now have Bolognese Sauce. Set aside.

3. In a strainer, drain the excess fat and liquid (This will remove the remaining fat and guarantee a creamy sauce). Set aside.

5. Cut eggplant into round ½"(1.27cm) thick slices. Grill eggplant discs over high heat until golden brown and grill-marks form (About 2 minutes per side).

6. Prepare white sauce by combining yogurt, ½ cup mozzarella, egg, chopped parsley, green onion and salt and pepper to taste.

7. Start building the layers by adding grilled eggplant, Bolognese Sauce, slices of ham, and white sauce until you fill the baking-dish almost to the top. Top the last layer with the white sauce and sprinkle the rest of the mozzarella cheese.

Calories	Protein	Carbs	sugar	Total Fat	Sat Fat	Fiber
323	38g	10g	3g	14g	5g	3g

CHEESEBURGER ROLL

Total time: 35 min.
Prep: 10 min.
Cook: 25 min.
Yield: 8 portions.

Ingredients:

2 lbs. (907 g) 93% lean ground beef.
1 tablespoon Worcestershire sauce.
1 tablespoon Dijon mustard.
2 teaspoons reduced sodium seasoned salt.
2 garlic cloves, minced.
½ yellow onion, chopped.
⅓ cup breadcrumbs.
½ cup parsley, chopped.

For the stuffing:

10 slices low-fat ham.
1 large carrot, shredded.
½ cup green onions, chopped.
1 cup pickles, chopped.
1 and ½ cups shredded low-fat Cheddar cheese.
½ cup celery, chopped.
1 large tomato, sliced.

Tips: If you prefer a different protein you can substitute the ground beef for ground chicken or turkey, bear in mind the nutritional values will vary.

1. Preheat oven to 425 °F (218 °C) and line a 10"x 12"(30cm x 25cm) baking tray with cling-film or wax paper.

2. In a large bowl, combine, meat, onions, garlic, mustard, seasoned salt, breadcrumbs, parsley, and Worcestershire sauce.

3. Mix until everything is well-combined. I like to use my clean bare hands for this job as it is much easier than trying to use a spoon.

4. On the lined baking-tray, spread out the meat mixture and pat it down to make it even.

5. Layer the ingredients for the stuffing starting with the ham.

6. Start wrapping the roll tight up to the middle, release the meat from the cling film and keep rolling, patting gently throughout the process.

7. Decorate the Cheeseburger Roll with slices of tomato on top and bake the roll until the tomatoes are slightly roasted. (About 25 minutes) Serve with whole grain burger buns.

Calories	Protein	Carbs	sugar	Total Fat	Sat Fat	Fiber
269	35g	8g	3g	10g	4g	1g

CAULIFLOWER SHEPHERD'S PIE

Total time: 35 min.
Prep: 20 min.
Cook: 15 min.
Yield: 5 servings.

Ingredients:

2 lbs. (907 g) 90% lean ground beef.
1 large yellow onion, chopped.
1 large carrot, diced.
2 garlic cloves, minced.
2 tablespoons tomato paste.
2 cups tomato sauce.
1 cup shelled edamame soybeans.
1 and ½ teaspoons reduced sodium seasoned salt.
¼ cup chopped parsley.

For the Topping:

1 large cauliflower head chopped into small florets.
¼ cup low-fat cheddar cheese.
1 egg.
1 and ½ tablespoons reduced-fat Parmesan cheese.

1. Preheat oven to 425 °F (218 °C) and lightly grease a 10" baking-dish (25 cm) with cooking-spray. Set aside.

2.

Chop cauliflower in small florets and cook in the microwave with ¼ cup of water for 7 minutes. Let it cool.

4.

Put the drained ground beef back into frying pan and add onions, carrots, garlic, tomato paste, tomato sauce, edamame and seasoned salt. Stir well.

3.

In a large nonstick frying pan over medium-high heat, cook ground beef, crumbling the meat with wood or plastic utensil while cooking to facilitate cooking and prevent clumps. Cook for about 5 minutes. In a strainer, drain the excess fat and liquid.

5.

Blend the precooked cauliflower until smooth.

6.

Thoroughly mix the cauliflower blend with the cheddar cheese, chopped parsley, and the egg.

7.

Cover the bottom of a 10"-dish with the meat, spreading evenly.

8.

Top with the cauliflower mash spreading carefully, finish with Parmesan cheese and bake it for 15 minutes or just until cauliflower begins to brown.

Calories	Protein	Carbs	sugar	Total Fat	Sat Fat	Fiber
424	48g	20g	9g	16g	6g	7g

CHEESE BURGER
WITH SAUSAGE, TURKEY BACON AND EGG

Total time: 25 min.
Prep: 10 min.
Cook: 15 min.
Yield: 4.

Ingredients:

1 lb. (453 g) ground beef 96% lean.
½ yellow onion, chopped.
1 teaspoon garlic, minced.
1 tablespoon yellow mustard.
1 tablespoon Worcestershire sauce.
½ cup lean turkey sausage, chopped.
¼ cup parsley, chopped.
1 teaspoon reduced sodium seasoned salt.
4 slices low-fat cheddar cheese.
4 small eggs.
4 slices lean turkey bacon.
4 Rye burger buns.

Garnishing:

Romaine lettuce.
Sliced tomatoes.
Pickles.

Tips: I use rye buns for this recipe but you may use any whole wheat/grain buns. Place buns in the oven for 3-4 minutes to warm up before making the burgers. The fries is on the sides section (pg. 123). If you can't find 96% ground beef, you may use 90-93%. Bear in mind that calories will increase.

1. Preheat oven to 425 °F (218 °C). Lightly grease a flat oven-pan.

2.
In a large bowl, combine ground beef, chopped onion, minced garlic, mustard, seasoned salt, chopped sausage, Worcestershire sauce, and chopped parsley. Mix until everything is well-combined. I like to use my bare hands for this job, as it is much easier than trying to use a large spoon.

3.
Divide meat mixture in four equal parts, using a cookie-cutter for each portion, and press down with a spoon making the burgers as shown in the photo or you can shape by hand if you prefer.

4.
Place the burgers on the greased pan and cook each side for 1 minute just to give them some color.

5.
Place cheddar cheese on top of each burger and place in the oven for 5 minutes just to melt the cheese and finish cooking the meat. 5 minutes will produce a medium burger, so adapt time to your preference but be careful to not over-cook as lean ground beef will easily dry up if cooked too long.

6.
While burgers are in the oven, start frying eggs in a nonstick frying pan greased with cooking-spray and on a microwave-safe dish lay down 2 sheets of paper towels, lay up the slices of bacon and cook it for 1 and ½ minutes or until they are crispy.

Calories	Protein	Carbs	sugar	Total Fat	Sat Fat	Fiber
450	45g	28g	6g	15g	4g	4g

CHILI CON CARNE

Total time: 30 min.
Prep: 15 min.
Cook: 15 min.
Yield: 6 portions.

Ingredients:

2 lbs. (907 g) 90% lean ground beef.
1 yellow onion.
3 garlic cloves.
3 tomatoes.
½ cup cilantro.
3 cups pinto beans, drained and rinsed.
1 and ½ teaspoons red chili flakes.
2 teaspoons reduced-sodium seasoned salt.
1 teaspoon paprika.
1 tablespoon tomato paste.
1 cup tomato sauce.
1 cup water.
½ cup green onions.
1 green bell pepper, chopped.
½ cup low-fat cheddar cheese.

TIPS: This recipe is mild. If you want it spicier add one more teaspoon of chili flakes

1.

Cook ground beef in a large, nonstick frying pan over medium-high heat. Crumble the meat in small pieces with wood or plastic utensil while cooking to facilitate cooking and prevent clumps. Cook for about 5 minutes.

3.

In a blender, add chopped tomatoes, onions, garlic, cilantro, paprika, chili flakes, tomato paste, seasoned salt and water. Blend until smooth for about 2 minutes.

2.

In a strainer, drain the excess fat and liquid.

4.

Return the beef to the frying pan and add the blended sauce and stir well.

5.

Add the tomato sauce, mix well.

6.

Add the drained pinto beans and the chopped bell-pepper.

7.

Cook for 5 more minutes to even out flavor. Finish by adding chopped green onions, cheese and sprinkled paprika on top.

Calories	Protein	Carbs	sugar	Total Fat	Sat Fat	Fiber
388	41g	28g	3g	12g	5g	9g

GRILLED PORK LOIN
WITH PEACH WEDGES

Total time: 30 min.
Prep: 15 min.
Cook: 15 min.
Yield: 8 portions.

Ingredients:

3 and ½ lbs.(1.5 kg) boneless pork loin.
3 garlic cloves, minced.
3 tablespoons balsamic vinegar.
2 teaspoons salt.
1 tablespoon dry thyme.
2 teaspoons black pepper.
1 tablespoon dry oregano.
3 tablespoons extra-virgin olive oil.
1 tablespoon Dijon mustard.
5 medium peaches.
Kitchen twine.

Tips: Serve this recipe with spicy potato wedges, recipe on sides section (pg.119). Also you can use beef tenderloin for this recipe if you don't like or can't eat pork.

1. Prepare grill or frying pan by lightly greasing with cooking-spray.

2.

With a sharp knife, trim away fat from pork loin by sliding the knife under the silvery skin as shown in the photo. Do this until you have a nice, pink loin without any white portions of fat.

4.

Cut a piece of kitchen twine long enough to tie each medallion individually to help it keep its shape when cooking.

3.

To cut loin medallions, use your large knife to cut 1.5" steaks, using your fingers to measure as shown in photo.

5.

Prepare the seasoning by mixing minced garlic, balsamic vinegar, salt, thyme, pepper, oregano, Dijon mustard, and extra-virgin olive oil. Mix well until well-combined.

6.

Brush seasoning over pork medallions on both sides.

7.

Preheat grill on medium-high heat, place pork medallions and let them grill for 15 minutes flipping every 4-5 minutes. If you have a cooking-thermometer, insert in the middle of medallions to check if they are cooked. The internal temperature should be 145 °F (62 °C), if you don't have one, just cut your biggest piece in the middle to check that it is fully cooked.

8.

5 minutes before pork cooking-time ends, cut peaches into wedges and grill them for 5 minutes, 2 and ½ minutes per side.

Calories	Protein	Carbs	sugar	Total Fat	Sat Fat	Fiber
382	52g	10g	8g	13g	3g	2g

PORK LOIN MILANESE
WITH APPLE CAULIFLOWER MASH AND LEMON SAUCE

Total time: 35 min.
Prep: 15 min.
Cook: 20 min.
Yield: 4 portions.

Ingredients:

4 boneless center-cut pork loin (1 and ½ lbs.) (680g), trimmed.
1 cup bread crumbs (whole grain preferable).
1 large egg.
1 teaspoon reduced sodium seasoned salt.

For apple cauliflower mash:

1 large green apple, peeled.
1 large cauliflower, in florets.
1 cup skimmed 2% milk.
1 tablespoon extra-virgin olive oil.
2 tablespoons parsley, chopped.
Salt and pepper to taste.

For lemon mustard sauce:

1 tablespoon Dijon mustard.
2 tablespoons lemon juice, freshly squeezed.
1 tablespoon extra-virgin olive oil.
¼ cup capers, drained.
A pinch of salt and pepper.

1. Preheat oven to 400 °F (204 °C) and lightly grease a baking-sheet with cooking-spray.

2.

Remove any visible fat from pork loins.

4.

In a large bowl, place pork loins, egg, and seasoned salt and mix well by hand.

3.

Place plastic wrap on bottom and top of meat and pound flat with the bottom of a pan, as shown in photo.

5.

Place pork Milanese in breadcrumbs, making sure all sides are evenly coated.

6.

Place the breaded pork on the prepared baking-sheet, spray cooking-spray on top of each Milanese and bake for 20-25 minutes or until golden-brown and pork is completely cooked through.

7.

Cut cauliflower into florets and peel apple and cut in mid size chunks. In a large microwave-safe bowl mix cauliflower florets, apple chunks, and 2 tablespoons of water. Cook for 3 minutes.

8.

In a blender, place cooked cauliflower and apple, add milk, olive oil, and blend until smooth. Season with salt and pepper and finish with chopped parsley. For the lemon sauce, mix lemon juice, olive oil, Dijon, salt and pepper. Mix well then add capers. Serve on top of pork Milanese.

Tips: You can substitute the pork loin for chicken breast or round steak if you don't like or can't eat pork.

Calories	Protein	Carbs	sugar	Total Fat	Sat Fat	Fiber
490	51g	32g	11g	17g	5g	5g

MINI BURGER PLATTER

Total time: 30 min.
Prep: 10 min.
Cook: 20 min.
Yield: 12 mini burgers. 2 servings

Ingredients:

1 and ½ lbs. (680 g) 93% lean ground beef.
1 tablespoon Dijon mustard.
1 tablespoon Worcestershire sauce.
1 teaspoon seasoning salt.
½ yellow onion, chopped.
1 teaspoon garlic powder.
2 tablespoons parsley, chopped.
10 baby Portobello mushrooms.
½ lb. (226g) Brussels sprout.
½ lb. (226g) asparagus.
1 large red onion, sliced.
15 cherry tomatoes.
2 medium carrots, chopped.

1.

In a large bowl, combine meat, onions, mustard, seasoned salt, parsley, garlic powder and Worcestershire sauce. Mix until everything is well-combined. I like to use my bare hands for this job, as it is much easier than trying to use a large spoon.

3.

Remove Brussels sprout bottom stems and cut in half. Chop carrots, remove asparagus stems and chop into large pieces, slice red onion thinly and slice baby mushroom. Start cooking by first placing carrots and Brussels sprouts in a large microwave-safe bowl with 2 tablespoons of water and microwave for 2 minutes. Set aside, do the same with the asparagus, cooking for 1 minute.

2.

Divide meat mixture in 12 equal parts using a cookie-cutter for each portion and press down with a spoon making the burgers as shown in the photo or you may shape by hand if you prefer.

4.

In a large bowl, place cooked vegetables and mix with sliced onions, tomatoes and sliced mushroom. Season with a drizzle of olive oil and salt and pepper to taste.

5.

In a pan, lightly greased with cooking-spray, cook mini-burgers for 2 minutes on each side. Be careful to not over-cook as lean ground beef will easily dry up if cooked too long. Serve burgers with a dollop of BBQ sauce (recipe is on sauces and dips section) or any sauce you prefer.

Calories	Protein	Carbs	sugar	Total Fat	Sat Fat	Fiber
466	53g	20g	9g	16g	0.2g	6g

MEDITERRANEAN BEEF ROLLS

Total time: 30 min.
Prep: 15 min.
Cook: 15 min.
Yield: 4 portions.

Ingredients:

4 thin-cut round steaks (1 and ½ lbs.) (680 g), trimmed.
4 slices lean turkey-bacon.
1 red bell pepper, sliced.
1 yellow bell pepper, sliced.
½ cup green olives, pitted.
1 cup baby carrots.
1 lb. (453g) fresh asparagus, trimmed.
½ teaspoon salt.
½ teaspoon.
½ black pepper.

For the sauce:

1 cup water.
2 tablespoons tomato paste.
1 tablespoon Dijon mustard.
2 tablespoons Worcestershire sauce.
1 teaspoon turmeric.

1.

Lay steaks out flat and trim any visible fat from the edges. If the steak is too thick, place plastic wrap on both sides of the meat and pound flat with the bottom of a pan as shown in the photo.

3.

Season steak with salt and pepper and start adding the stuffing (bell peppers, asparagus, carrots, and olives).

2.

Start building the rolls by placing each flat steak on top of a bacon rasher.

4.

Roll up tightly (like rolling a rug). Secure each roll with a toothpick or tie with twine.

5.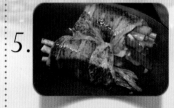

Preheat a frying pan over high heat, lightly spray with cooking-spray and stir-fry rolls for 1 minute on each side until they are uniformly brown as shown in photo. Remove rolls from pan and set aside.

6.

In the same frying pan, add water, Dijon, tomato paste, Worcestershire sauce, turmeric and the remaining vegetables and olives. Place rolls on top of vegetables.

7.

Cover, reduce the heat to medium and let cook for 3 minutes (for medium), or 5 minutes (for medium well), adding more water if needed.

Tips: You may substitute the water with beef stock and you may also add more vegetables to the recipe to make this plate even heartier.

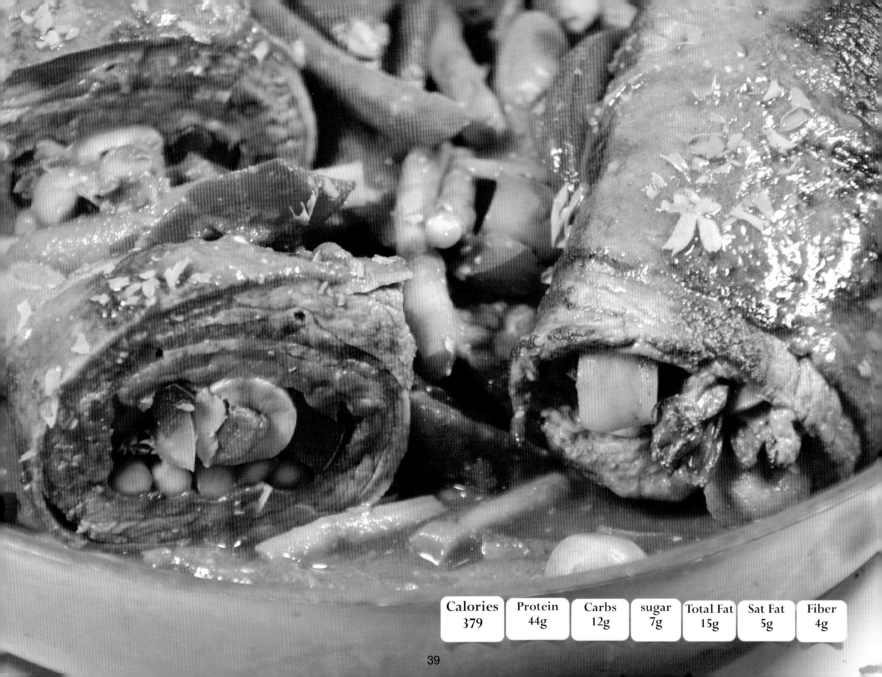

Calories	Protein	Carbs	sugar	Total Fat	Sat Fat	Fiber
379	44g	12g	7g	15g	5g	4g

BACHELOR BOLOGNESE

Total time: 20 min.
Prep: 7 min.
Cook: 13 min.
Yield: 4 portions.

Ingredients:

½ package whole grain linguine.
12 oz. (340 g) lean beef.
3 larges tomatoes.
10 cherry tomatoes, halved.
1 medium yellow onion.
4 garlic cloves, peeled.
¼ cup green olives, pitted.
1 tablespoon tomato paste.
1 and ½ cups light tomato sauce.
1 cube beef bouillon.
2 tablespoons dry parsley.
4 tablespoons low-fat Parmesan cheese.
1 tablespoon extra-virgin olive oil.
Fresh basil leaves.

1.

Bring large pot of water to boil (no salt needed). Add spaghetti and cook for 8 to 10 minutes or until al dente; drain and set aside.

2.

Roughly chop tomatoes and onion. Set aside.

6.

Drizzle 1 tablespoon extra-virgin olive oil to the cooked linguine, salt and pepper to taste, dry parsley, and mix well.

3.

Cut beef into small cubes and cut onion into chunks. (Remove any visible fat)

4.

In a blender, blend beef cubes, chopped tomatoes, onion, garlic, olives, tomato paste, tomato sauce, handful of basil leaves, beef bouillon, and blend for 10 seconds, just enough to breakdown the meat.

7.

In the same pan, combine cooked spaghetti with Bolognese, mixing well. Serve with parmesan cheese and basil leaves.

5.
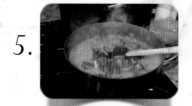
In a medium sauce pan over medium high heat, mix blended Bolognese with the cherry tomatoes and cook for 15 minutes.

Calories	Protein	Carbs	sugar	Total Fat	Sat Fat	Fiber
492	44g	56g	12g	15g	2g	9g

POULTRY

CHICKEN PIBIL TACOS

Total time: 40 min.
Prep: 10 min.
Cook: 30 min.
Yield: 6 servings.

Ingredients:

2 lbs. (907 g) boneless, skinless chicken breast.
12 whole-wheat (Low carb) tortillas.

For the Pibil sauce:

1 and ½ tablespoons achiote paste.
1 cup freshly-squeezed orange juice.
½ cup freshly-squeezed lime juice.
3 cups chicken broth.
1 teaspoon dry oregano.
½ teaspoon cumin.
½ teaspoon ground allspice.
1 and ½ teaspoons kosher salt.
½ teaspoon black pepper.
2 tomatoes, roughly chopped.
1 yellow onion, roughly chopped.
3 garlic cloves.

For the pickled red-onion:

1 red onion, thinly sliced.
½ teaspoon black pepper, ground.
½ teaspoon kosher salt.
1 teaspoon dry oregano.
1 teaspoon garlic, diced.
1 and ½ cups red-wine vinegar.
¼ cup cilantro, chopped.

1. Cut chicken breasts into bite-size cubes (about 1"x 1")
(2 cm) while removing any remaining fat.

2.

Place all ingredients for the Pibil sauce in a large blender or food processor and blend until smooth.

3.

In a large bowl, pour the marinade mixture over the chicken cubes and mix well.

6.

Peel and thinly slice the onion, dice the garlic and chop cilantro finely.

4.

Bring the chicken and sauce to a simmer at medium heat and let cook for about 20 minutes.

5.

Cook for an additional 10 minutes until the sauce thickens. Finish with chopped cilantro and it`s ready to serve.

7.

Mix the sliced onions with the remaining ingredients and place a small amount on top of the chicken. You can serve with guacamole as well. (Recipe is on pg. 150.)

Tips: You can make the same recipe using pork loin or lean beef. bear in mind the nutritional values will vary.

Calories	Protein	Carbs	sugar	Total Fat	Sat Fat	Fiber
449	53g	35g	6g	5g	1g	16g

BAKED CHICKEN FINGERS

Total time: 35 min.
Prep: 10 min.
Cook: 25 min.
Yield: 4 portions.

Ingredients:

1 and ½ lbs. (680 g) skinless, boneless chicken breast.
2 eggs.
1 cups bread crumbs (whole grain preferable).
⅓ cup almond meal/flour.
1 tablespoon paprika.
½ teaspoon cayenne pepper.(optional)
1 tablespoon lemon pepper.
1 tablespoon seasoned salt.
1 teaspoon baking-powder.
½ cup fresh parsley chopped.
2 tablespoons salt-free seasoning.

For the dipping sauce:

1 (5oz) container plain fat-free Greek yogurt.
2 tablespoons Dijon mustard.
¼ cup hot-sauce for wings.

1. Preheat oven to 425 °F (218 °C). Grease baking-sheet with nonstick cooking-spray and set aside.

2.
In a frying pan over medium-high heat, toss and cook breadcrumbs and almond flour for about 2 minutes until gently browned.

3.
In a large plate, mix all the dry ingredients and add the chopped parsley.

6.
Place the breaded chicken on the prepared baking-sheet, spray cooking-spray on top of each strip and bake for 20-25 minutes or until golden brown and chicken is completely cooked through.

4.
Using a sharp knife, slice the chicken breasts horizontally into two even pieces then cut into 4 strips. (Remove any visible fat).

5.
Lightly beat the eggs and dip chicken in the egg wash, then place into the seasoned breadcrumbs, making sure all sides are evenly coated with breadcrumbs.

7.
Combine the 3 dipping-sauce ingredients, mix well and serve.

Tips: You can substitute chicken breast for chicken loin or turkey breast.

Calories	Protein	Carbs	sugar	Total Fat	Sat Fat	Fiber
457	64g	17g	2g	12g	2g	3g

BAKED BUFFALO WINGS

Total time: 55 min.
Prep: 15 min.
Cook: 40 min.
Yield: 4 portions.

Ingredients:

24 medium chicken wings.
1 cup light rye flour.
1 tablespoon paprika.
½ teaspoon cayenne pepper.
2 tablespoons onion powder.
1 teaspoon baking-powder.
2 tablespoons low-sodium seasoned salt.
1 cup buffalo sauce for wings.
2 tablespoons parsley (optional).

For the dipping sauce:

2 (5oz)containers plain fat-free yogurt.
¼ cup reduced-fat bleu cheese.
1 teaspoon garlic, minced.
1 teaspoon low-sodium soy sauce.

1. Preheat oven to 425 °F (218 °C). Line a baking-sheet with aluminum foil or a baking rack, lightly grease with cooking-spray and set aside.

2. Using a sharp knife, trim off any excess fat from wings.

4. Mix the flour, baking-powder and seasonings.

3. Before seasoning, pat wings dry with paper towels.

5. Place the previous mix in a re-sealable plastic bag and add wings, close the bag and shake it until wings are fully coated. Remove excess flour and place wings in the prepared baking-sheet.

6. Bake the wings in the middle of the oven for 20 minutes on each side or until you see significant browning and crisping on the skin. Once the wings are done and crispy, coat the wings in the buffalo sauce tossing them in a large bowl. Optionally, top with chopped parsley.

7. In the microwave, melt the bleu cheese for 10 seconds, add the remaining ingredients for the dipping sauce mix well and serve.

Calories	Protein	Carbs	sugar	Total Fat	Sat Fat	Fiber
587	70g	13g	2g	28g	9g	1g

Total time: 40 min.
Prep: 15 min.
Cook: 25 min.
Yield: 4 servings.

Ingredients:

2 lbs. (907g) boneless, skinless chicken-breast.
1 red, 1 green and 1 yellow bell pepper.
1 red onion.
Skewers (8).

For the Marinade:

1 (5oz) container plain fat-free Greek yogurt.
1 tablespoon extra-virgin olive oil.
1 teaspoon paprika.
½ teaspoon cumin.
1 pinch ground cinnamon.
1 pinch cayenne pepper (optional).
Zest of one lemon.
3 tablespoons lime juice.

For the Tabbouleh:

¼ cup fine #1 bulgur wheat.
2 large tomatoes, diced.
1 large cucumber, diced.
½ cup parsley, chopped.
½ cup green onions, chopped.
½ bunch chopped mint (optional).
2 tablespoons extra-virgin olive oil.
¼ cup lemon juice. (1 large lemon)
¼ cup lime juice. (2 medium limes)
Salt and pepper to taste.

1. Preheat grill to medium-high heat.

2.

Very finely chop tomatoes, cucumber, herbs and green onions. In large bowl, place all tabbouleh ingredients and mix well. Season with salt and pepper to taste.

3.

Let mixture set for 10 minutes before serving.

4.

Cut chicken into 1 and ½" cubes and season with salt and pepper. Cut bell peppers lengthwise on all four sides to make four strips from each pepper. Cut across strips to create 1" squares.

5.

Mix marinade ingredients and set aside. (Reserve part of the marinate to serve as sauce on top of each kebab.)

6.

Brush kebabs with marinade making sure all pieces are completely coated.

7.

Preheat grill to high heat. Grill kebabs turning occasionally for 10-12 minutes or until meat is thoroughly cooked.

Tips: You can use any other type of protein such as beef, lean lamb or even pieces of vegetables for a vegetarian option.

Calories	Protein	Carbs	sugar	Total Fat	Sat Fat	Fiber
458	61g	14g	7g	15g	2g	4g

51

TURKEY KEBABS

Total time: 22 min.
Prep: 10 min.
Cook: 12 min.
Yield: 2 servings.

Ingredients:

1 lb. (453 g) boneless, skinless turkey-breast.
½ tablespoon Cajun seasoning.
½ tablespoon Italian seasoning.
1 tablespoon extra-virgin olive oil.
1 teaspoon salt.
½ teaspoon pepper.
Chopped parsley (for garnishing).
10 Green olives stuffed with garlic.
10 Grape tomatoes.
4 lemons, grilled.
Bamboo Skewers.

1. Preheat grill to medium-high heat.

Trim off any excess fat and cut turkey breast into large bite-size pieces (about 1″).(2 cm).

4.

Start building kebabs by adding 1 piece of turkey breast, 1 grape tomato and 1 olive to each bamboo skewer.

3.

In a medium bowl, combine turkey pieces with Cajun seasoning, Italian seasoning, olive oil, salt, pepper, and mix well.

5.

Prepare lemons for grilling by cutting in half and removing any visible seeds.

6.

Spray cooking-spray on grill and cook kebabs for 2 minutes on each side totaling 8 minutes. Grill lemons cut-side-down until charred (about 3 minutes).

7.

Remove kebabs and lemons from grill; squeeze lemons liberally onto kebabs and serve.

TIPS: You can use any other type of protein such as beef, lean lamb or even pieces of vegetables for a vegetarian option.

Calories	Protein	Carbs	sugar	Total Fat	Sat Fat	Fiber
417	69g	5g	0.4g	11g	1g	0.4g

PULLED CHICKEN
WITH MASALA SAUCE AND CUCUMBER MANGO SALSA

Total time: 35 min.
Prep: 15 min.
Cook: 20 min.
Yield: 6 portions.

Ingredients:

1 and ½ lbs. (680 g) cooked skinless, boneless chicken breast.
6 whole grain burger buns or 3 naan breads.

For the Masala sauce:

1 tablespoon tomato paste.
1 yellow onion, diced.
4 garlic cloves.
2 teaspoons cumin.
1 teaspoon salt.
1 tablespoon ginger paste or fresh ginger.
1 pinch cayenne pepper
½ teaspoon ground cinnamon.
1 teaspoon yellow curry.
2 large tomatoes, chopped.
Juice of one lime (about 2 tablespoons).
1 cup plain fat-free Greek yogurt.
½ cup cilantro with stem.

For the cucumber mango salsa:

1 large cucumber, sliced.
½ red onion, finely sliced.
2 tablespoons cilantro, chopped.
1 large mango, peeled and cut into small cubes.
1 tablespoon extra-virgin olive oil.
Salt and pepper to taste.

1. Heat a large frying pan over medium heat. Cook onions for 2 minutes.

3. Place the previously cooked Masala mixture in a blender or food processor; add the cilantro and blend until smooth (about 5 minutes).

2. In the same pan, add garlic, tomato paste, cumin, salt, ginger paste, cayenne pepper, cinnamon, curry, and chopped tomatoes to the onions. Cook for 3 more minutes.

4. Add Greek yogurt to blended mix and blend for another 2 minutes.

5. Thinly slice the cooked chicken breast and add Masala sauce to taste.

6. For the cucumber mango salsa; mix all the ingredients together and add extra virgin olive oil, salt and pepper to taste.

TIPS: This recipe also can be served with Naan bread, brown rice or quinoa or just with the cucumber mango salsa on the side.

Calories	Protein	Carbs	sugar	Total Fat	Sat Fat	Fiber
381	32g	38g	16g	11g	2g	5g

Calories with naan bread.

YELLOW CURRY CHICKEN LEGS

Total time: 45 min.
Prep: 10 min.
Cook: 35 min.
Yield: 6 portions.

Ingredients:

12 skinless chicken drumsticks.
6 skinless chicken thighs.
2 cans chickpeas drained (2 lbs.).
1 cup uncooked brown rice.
Salt and pepper.
1 Cup fat-free plain Greek yogurt.
¼ Cilantro, chopped.

For the Yellow Curry Sauce:

1 low-sodium chicken bouillon.
1 medium red onion.
1 large yellow onion.
3 gloves garlic.
1 tablespoon ginger paste (or chopped fresh ginger).
2 green bell peppers (cut and seeds removed).
½ bunch fresh cilantro.
1 teaspoon turmeric.
2 teaspoons curry powder.
2 tablespoons tomato paste.

1.

Season both sides of chicken legs with salt and pepper to taste.

3.

In a blender, blend all ingredients for yellow curry sauce until smooth. About 2 minutes.

2.

On very hot nonstick pan, brown chicken legs for approximately 2 minutes on each side.

4.

In a deep pan, place curry sauce, browned chicken legs, and brown rice. Cook uncovered on medium-low heat for 30 minutes, stirring occasionally.

5.

Add chickpeas during last 5 minutes of cooking. Remove from heat.

6.

Add 1 dollop of fat-free Greek yogurt to each chicken leg, garnish with cilantro leaves and spoon to serve.

Calories	Protein	Carbs	sugar	Total Fat	Sat Fat	Fiber
482	31g	36g	4g	6g	1g	5g

CAULIFLOWER PIZZA CRUST

Total time: 40 min.
Prep: 10 min.
Cook: 30 min.
Yield: 6 slices.

Ingredients:

1 cauliflower head.
1 tablespoon herbes de Provence or dry oregano.
½ teaspoon kosher salt.
1 teaspoon onion powder.
1 cup low-fat grated mozzarella cheese.
2 eggs.

For the Topping:

1 tablespoon tomato paste.
3 tablespoons water.
12 cherry tomatoes, cut in half.
1 lb. (453 g) cooked chicken breast, shredded.
½ can heart of palm, chopped.
12 green olives.
1 cup baby spinach.
½ yellow onion, sliced.
½ cup low-fat mozzarella cheese, grated.

1. Preheat oven to 450 °F (232 °C). Lightly coat baking-sheet with high-heat baking-spray and set aside.

2.

Break cauliflower into florets and pulse in food processor or blender until finely chopped.

4.

In a bowl, combine cauliflower with mozzarella, oregano, salt, onion powder and eggs. Mix well. Transfer resulting dough to center of baking-sheet.

3.

In microwave-safe bowl, cook cauliflower for 6 minutes or until tender. Place cauliflower in towel, and squeeze out excess water making sure it is completely dry.

5.

Pat the dough down thoroughly so it is tight and even. Don't make crust too thick or too thin.

6.

Bake crust 20 minutes. If after 20 minutes, crust is still soggy, bake additional 5-10 minutes before adding topping.

7.

Dilute tomato paste with 3 tablespoons water and spread over crust.

8.

Spread topping ingredients in layers: chicken, chopped heart of palm, sliced cherry tomato halves, green olives, sliced onion and mozzarella cheese. Place back in oven and bake for additional 10 minutes. Remove pizza, spread baby spinach on top and serve.

Calories	Protein	Carbs	sugar	Total Fat	Sat Fat	Fiber
243	26g	15g	9g	9g	2g	3g

CHICKEN PARMIGIANA

Total time: 30 min.
Prep time: 15 min.
Cook: 15 min.
Yield: 3 portions.

Ingredients:

3 large boneless, skinless chicken breasts.
1 teaspoons chicken-flavor bouillon powder.
2 eggs (lightly beaten).
⅔ cup breadcrumbs.
1 cup tomato sauce.
6 slices lean Black Forest ham.
6 slices provolone cheese.

For the Topping:

1 large tomato.
12 black olives, sliced.
1 tablespoon dry oregano.
Basil leaves.

1. Preheat oven to 400 °F (204 °C). Slightly grease baking-sheet with high-heat cooking-spray and set aside.

2. Cut chicken breasts in halves and remove any excess of fat.

3. Season chicken on both sides with chicken bouillon powder or salt and pepper.

4. Dip chicken in egg mix; let excess drip off.

5. Completely cover both sides with breadcrumbs.

6. Lightly grease nonstick frying pan with cooking-spray and heat on medium-high; place breaded chicken pieces in pan and sear for one minute on each side.

7. Place breaded chicken on greased baking-sheet. Start building parmigiana by layering ham, tomato sauce.

8. Next add cheese slice, olives, tomato slice and dry oregano to each piece. Place in preheated oven and bake 15 minutes. Serve with a fresh basil leaf on top of each serving.

Calories	Protein	Carbs	sugar	Total Fat	Sat Fat	Fiber
343	49g	11g	3g	10g	1g	2g

CHICKEN & SAUSAGE GUMBO

WITH GARBANZO BEANS

Total time: 35 min.
Prep: 10 min.
Cook: 25 min.
Yield: 7 portions.

Ingredients:

2 lbs. (907g) boneless, skinless chicken-breast.

7 oz. (198g) 60% reduced-fat smoked turkey sausage.

2 cans reduced sodium garbanzo beans (chickpeas).

2 large tomatoes.

1 large yellow onion.

4 garlic cloves.

2 tablespoons dried oregano.

1 teaspoon black pepper.

½ teaspoon cayenne pepper (optional).

2 teaspoons paprika.

½ cup cilantro leaves with stems.

1 and ½ teaspoons low-sodium chicken bouillon.

3 cups water.

3 cups frozen okra.

1 cup frozen sweet corn.

1.

In a blender, place tomatoes, half onion, garlic, oregano, black pepper, cayenne, paprika, chicken bouillon, half-cup garbanzo beans, cilantro, and three cups water and blend for 3 minutes until smooth. Set aside.

3.

Cut chicken breasts into cubes and season with salt and pepper.

2.

Slice sausage into thin discs.

4.

Place chicken in large, deep-dish sauté-pan (with cover) and cook uncovered on medium-high heat for 3 minutes. Add sausage followed by remaining chopped onion and cook 2 additional minutes.

5.

Add sauce to chicken and sausage and stir well.

6.

Add okra, remaining garbanzo beans and sweet corn.

7.

Cover and let cook for 20 minutes, stirring occasionally.

Calories	Protein	Carbs	sugar	Total Fat	Sat Fat	Fiber
410	41g	38g	4g	9g	2g	9g

ASIAN PEANUT SAUCE CHICKEN

WITH VIBRANT SPAGHETTI

Total time: 40 min.
Prep: 20 min.
Cook: 20 min.
Yield: 5 portions.

Ingredients:

10 chicken thighs. (Skinless preferable)

For the Sauce:

⅓ cup low-fat smooth peanut butter.
½ cup lite coconut milk.
1 medium onion, chopped.
2 garlic cloves, diced.
2 and ½ cups of hot water.
½ cup cilantro leaves.
½ teaspoon kosher salt.
½ teaspoon black pepper.
1 tablespoon turmeric.
⅓ teaspoon cayenne pepper (optional).

For the Spaghetti:

½ package whole grain spaghetti.
1 large carrot, shredded.
1 cup broccoli, cut into small florets.
1 cup snow peas, halved.
1 tablespoon extra-virgin olive oil.
½ tablespoon soy sauce.
2 tablespoons roasted peanuts, chopped.
1 red chili-pepper, sliced.
1 tablespoon sesame seeds.

1. Bring large pot of water to boil (no salt needed) and cook spaghetti for 8 to 10 minutes or until al dente; drain and set aside.

2.
Remove chicken skin and trim any visible fat. Season with salt and pepper. If using skinless thighs also remove any visible fat.

3.
Sear chicken thighs over medium-high heat for 2 minutes each side. Set aside.

4.
Shred carrot, chop broccoli in florets and cut snow peas in half.

5.
Microwave snow peas 1 minute in a microwave safe bowl with one tablespoon of water.

6.
Combine all ingredients for the sauce and blend until smooth.

7.
Add sauce to chicken and let it cook on medium-high heat for 20 minutes.

8.
In large pan, heat olive oil, add vegetables, cooked spaghetti, and soy sauce and finish up with salt, pepper and sesame seeds. Place serving-size spaghetti on plates, add chicken and sauce. Garnish with chopped peanuts and sliced red chili pepper and serve

Calories	Protein	Carbs	sugar	Total Fat	Sat Fat	Fiber
554	40g	35g	5g	22g	5g	6g

CRISPY OVEN UNFRIED CHICKEN
WITH KIWI SYRUP AND JALAPEÑO CORNBREAD WAFFLES

Total time: 45 min.
Prep time: 15 min.
Cook: 30 min.
Yield: 5 portions.

Ingredients:

2 large bone-in skinless chicken-breasts.
4 skinless chicken drumsticks.
4 skinless chicken thighs.
2 eggs.
1 tablespoon Tabasco sauce.
½ cup fat-free Greek yogurt.

Spice Flour Mix:

½ cup rye flour.
2 teaspoons paprika.
1 tablespoon chicken flavor bouillon powder.
1 tablespoon ranch dressing powder.
½ teaspoon turmeric.
2 teaspoons baking-powder.
1 tablespoon garlic powder.
½ cup breadcrumbs.
¼ uncooked couscous.

Kiwi syrup:

2 large very ripe kiwis.
1 tablespoon light agave or ½-teaspoon stevia.
1 tablespoon water.

1. Preheat oven to 400 °F (200 °C). Lightly spray high-heat cooking-spray over wire grating-pan or baking-sheet and set aside.

2.

Remove skin and trim any excess fat from chicken.

4.

In large bowl, place chicken and pour egg mixture over it. Using your hands, make sure all chicken parts are thoroughly coated with mixture.

3.

Lightly beat eggs, add Tabasco sauce and yogurt and mix well.

5.

Mix all Spice Flour ingredients on a plate and roll each chicken part thoroughly in flour mixture to make sure it sticks to chicken.

6.

Arrange chicken parts on grill-rack or baking pan. Bake 30 minutes, turning once after 15 minutes.

7.

Peel kiwi and dice finely; add water and cook for 1 minute in microwave.

8.

Add agave or stevia, mix well and serve kiwi sauce to taste over baked chicken.

Calories	Protein	Carbs	sugar	Total Fat	Sat Fat	Fiber
471	54g	34g	8g	11g	3g	3g

Per 2 pieces with sauce

JALAPEÑO CORNBREAD WAFFLES

Total time: 15 min.
Prep: 5 min.
Cook: 10 min.
Yield: 5 small waffles.

Ingredients:

½ cup unsweetened almond milk.
2 cups yellow corn, drained.
2 large eggs.
⅓ cup yellow corn meal.
½ cup brown rice flour.
½ teaspoon baking-powder.
1 tablespoon reduced-fat grated Parmesan cheese.
½ teaspoon salt.
½ teaspoon pepper.
½ tablespoon extra-virgin olive oil.
½ cup green onion, chopped.
2 jalapeños, chopped.

1. Preheat a waffle iron on medium high heat.

2. In a blender, place almond milk, 1 cup yellow corn, eggs, corn meal, flour, Parmesan, olive oil, baking-powder and salt and pepper. Blend for 2 minutes until smooth.

4. In a large bowl, place waffle-mixture, the remaining cup of corn, chopped green onion and chopped jalapeños. Mix well until fully combined.

3. With the tip of a knife, cut Jalapeño lengthwise and remove the middle stem containing the seeds. Discard seeds, putting some aside in case you want your waffles a bit spicy. Finely dice jalapeño and set aside.

5. Spray cooking-spray over preheated waffle iron, and pour mix into cavities, cooking until golden-brown on both sides. Serve hot.

Calories	Protein	Carbs	sugar	Total Fat	Sat Fat	Fiber
233	7g	40g	3g	5g	0.7g	3g

Per waffle

69

TURKEY RICOTTA LASAGNA ROLLS

Total time: 35 min.
Prep: 20 min.
Cook: 15 min.
Yield: 6 portions.

Ingredients:

6 whole-grain lasagna-sheets.
1 lb. (453g) lean, ground turkey.
1 green bell pepper, chopped.
½ yellow onion, chopped.
1 and ½ tablespoons Dijon mustard.
1 teaspoon garlic powder.
1 cup tomato sauce.
½ tablespoon paprika.
¼ cup basil, chopped.
2 cups low-fat ricotta cheese.
1 large egg.
2 cups spinach, chopped.
1 tablespoon Italian seasoning.
½ teaspoon low-sodium seasoned salt.
1 tablespoon reduced fat grated Parmesan.

1. Preheat oven to 400 °F (204 °C) and lightly grease a baking-sheet with cooking-spray. Set aside.

2.

In a large pot, bring water to a boil and cook lasagna in water for 8 to 10 minutes. Drain and set aside.

4.

Over medium-high heat, first stir-fry chopped onion and bell pepper for 2 minutes. Add the ground turkey, crumbling the meat into small pieces with wood or plastic utensil while cooking to facilitate cooking and prevent clumps.

3.

Chop onion and bell pepper in small pieces.

5.

While the meat is cooking, start chopping the spinach and basil.

6.

In a medium bowl, mix ricotta cheese, egg, chopped spinach, chopped basil and a pinch of salt and black pepper.

7.

Once the meat is cooked, add the spices, the tomato sauce and the Dijon mustard. Stir and mix well.

8.

In a baking-sheet, lay out lasagna-sheets and then spread a layer of ricotta mixture onto the sheets. Add the turkey mixture next and spread evenly. Roll the lasagna sheet up starting at one end of each then arrange in a baking pan. Bake for 15 minutes. Serve with grated Parmesan on top and one basil-leaf.

Calories	Protein	Carbs	sugar	Total Fat	Sat Fat	Fiber
328	26g	27g	7g	10g	3g	5g

71

HASSELBACK CHICKEN
WITH CREAMY SPINACH STUFFING

Total time: 35 min.
Prep: 10 min.
Cook: 25 min.
Yield: 4 portions.

Ingredients:

4 skinless, boneless chicken-breasts, about 8 oz.(226g) each.
2 slices turkey bacon.
½ teaspoon paprika.
½ teaspoon salt.
½ teaspoon black pepper.
½ teaspoon onion powder.

For the creamy spinach:

2 garlic gloves, minced.
1 cup low-fat 2% cottage cheese.
2 cups spinach.
1 teaspoon yellow mustard.

1. Preheat oven to 400 °F (204 °C) and lightly grease baking-sheet with cooking-spray and set side.

2. In a microwave-safe dish, lay down 2 sheets of paper towels, lay the slices of bacon and microwave for 1 and ½ minutes or until crispy.

4. Over medium-high heat, lightly greased with cooking spray stir-fry spinach and garlic, then add the cottage cheese and cook for about 1 minute. Turn off heat.

3. Carefully cut 6 slits about ½" (1.27cm) apart across each chicken breast about ¾" (1cm) deep, making sure not to cut all the way through.

5. Drain the stuffing and mix the liquid with 1 teaspoon yellow mustard. This will be your sauce.

6. Stuff each of the slits in the chicken with the creamy spinach and transfer to baking-sheet.

7. Mix all the seasonings and sprinkle over each chicken breast. Bake for 20-25 minutes or until chicken juices run clear from slits.

8. Chop the bacon and sprinkle over the chicken just before serving.

Calories	Protein	Carbs	sugar	Total Fat	Sat Fat	Fiber
360	59g	4g	2g	11g	4g	1g

SEAFOOD

SEAFOOD MAC & CHEESE

Total time: 35 min.
Prep: 15 min.
Cook: 20 min.
Yield: 6 portions.

Ingredients:

2 cups whole-grain pasta elbows (Uncooked).
1 lb. (453g) jumbo shrimp, peeled and deveined.
½ lb. (226g) crabmeat, cooked.
½ lb. (226g) lobster meat, cooked.
1 medium yellow onion, chopped.
1 green bell pepper, chopped.
½ cup green onions, chopped.
1 large tomato, chopped.
½ cup fresh cilantro leaves, chopped.
3 garlic cloves, minced.
1 cup reduced-fat cream cheese.
1 cup sharp cheddar cheese.
2 teaspoons cornstarch.
1/3 cup 2% reduced-fat milk.
1 and ½ teaspoons seafood seasoning.

1. Preheat oven to 400 °F (204 °C). Lightly grease nonstick baking-pan with cooking-spray.

2. Fill a large pot with hot water, add 1 teaspoon salt and bring to a boil. Add pasta to water and cook according to pasta package directions. While pasta is cooking, start chopping bell pepper, onion, tomato, cilantro, green onions and mince garlic.

4. In the same pan, add crab meat, lobster meat, shrimps, chopped cilantro, chopped green onions and chopped tomato. Stir and mix all ingredients and let it cook for 3 minutes.

3. Preheat a nonstick frying pan over medium-high heat, lightly grease with cooking spray and add chopped onions, bell pepper and minced garlic, let it cook for 2 minutes.

5. In a small bowl, dilute cornstarch with milk, making sure there are no lumps. Then add to the seafood mixture and stir. Continue by adding the cream cheese and finish up with seafood seasoning. Mix well until combined and creamy. Let cook for another 3 minutes.

6. Drain the pasta but save ⅓ cup of the water for later. Take the drained pasta, add the water you saved and add a drizzle of extra-virgin olive oil (optional). In a large bowl, Place pasta in a large bowl and pour the seafood mixture over it, mixing well until all ingredients are combined.

7. Grease a baking dish large enough to hold the pasta. Spread evenly. Top with cheddar cheese and bake for 20 minutes.

Calories	Protein	Carbs	sugar	Total Fat	Sat Fat	Fiber
448	40g	38g	6g	14g	7g	2g

CAJUN JAMBALAYA RICE

Total time: 35 min.
Prep: 15 min.
Cook: 20 min.
Yield: 7 portions.

Ingredients:

2 lbs. (907 g) skinless, boneless chicken breast.
16 large shrimps, peeled and deveined.
7 ounces (198 g) low-fat turkey sausage.
2 cups fast-cook brown rice.
1 large yellow onion, chopped.
1 large green pepper, chopped.
3 medium tomatoes, chopped.
1 cup frozen yellow corn.
1 jalapeño chili, seeded and minced.
2 tablespoons Worcestershire sauce.
2 teaspoons hot sauce.
3 and ½ cups of water.
½ cup cilantro, chopped.
½ cup green onions, chopped.
2 teaspoons Cajun seasoning.
1 teaspoon salt.
½ teaspoon pepper.

1. Over medium-high heat, preheat grill or frying pan, lightly greased with cooking-spray.

2.
Cut sausage in ½-inch thick slices (1 cm) and cut chicken in bite-size cubes. Season chicken and shrimp with ½ teaspoon salt and ½ teaspoon pepper on both sides then place on grill/frying pan and cook for 2 minutes on each side just to give them a little color. Set aside.

4.
Pour 3 and ½ cups hot water into pan and turn the heat on medium high.

3.
In a large pan, add chopped tomatoes, chopped onion, minced jalapeño, chopped green pepper, corn, hot sauce, Cajun seasoning, Worcestershire sauce, ½ teaspoon salt, ½ teaspoon pepper and 2 cups of rice. Mix well.

5.
Add precooked chicken and sausage mixing well with all the other ingredients and let it cook for 15 minutes.

6.
Add precooked shrimp on top.

7.
Cover the pan and let it cook for 5 more minutes. Before serving, add chopped cilantro and chopped green onion on top giving a little stir. Serve right away.

Tips: If you can't find fast-cook brown rice follow the cooking directions from rice packaging. Normally regular brown rice is cooked in 25-30 minutes. For a vegetarian option substitute meats for chopped vegetables.

Calories	Protein	Carbs	sugar	Total Fat	Sat Fat	Fiber
471	43g	53g	5g	8g	2g	4g

CATFISH TACOS
WITH CREAMY GREEN APPLE COLESLAW

Total time: 25 min.
Prep: 15 min.
Cook: 10 min.
Yield: 12 tacos, 4 servings.

Ingredients:

2 and ½ lbs. skinless catfish filets.
Juice of 1 large lime (3 tablespoons).
1 tablespoon garlic minced.
¼ cup fresh cilantro, chopped.
½ teaspoon salt.
½ teaspoon pepper.
1 teaspoon turmeric.
12 whole grain (low carb) tortillas.

For the coleslaw:

2 radishes, thinly sliced.
1 and ½ cups red cabbage, shaved.
1 and ½ cups green cabbage, shaved.
½ yellow onion, sliced.
1 large carrot, shredded.
1 green apple, shredded with skin.
1 teaspoon apple-cider vinegar.
½ cup low-fat plain Greek yogurt.
1 tablespoon extra virgin olive oil.
½ teaspoon salt.
½ teaspoon pepper.

1.

Cut catfish fillets into small, bite-size squares. In a large bowl, add catfish, lemon juice, garlic, chopped cilantro, turmeric, salt and pepper mix and let it marinate for 5 minutes.

3.

Preheat a nonstick frying pan over medium-high heat (no grease needed as catfish will start to render its own fat). Cook for 5 minutes turning carefully approximately every minute.

2.

In a large bowl, place shaved cabbages, sliced radish, sliced onion, shredded carrot, shredded green apple, yogurt, vinegar, salt and pepper. Mix well until well-combined. Set aside in the refrigerator.

4.

Preheat a grill or separate frying pan and warm up the tortillas for about 30 seconds each side. For quicker results, you may microwave them for 10 seconds instead.

5.

Serve 2 tablespoons of cooked catfish over tortilla and 2 tablespoons of creamy slaw on top as shown in the photo.

Tips: You can use other fish for this recipe such as tilapia, salmon or even shrimp.

Calories	Protein	Carbs	sugar	Total Fat	Sat Fat	Fiber
217	25g	12g	4g	6g	1g	9g

Calories per taco.

LOADED SWEET POTATO SKINS

Total time: 30 min.
Prep: 15 min.
Cook: 15 min.
Yield: 4 servings.

Ingredients:

2 medium sweet-potatoes, halved.
1 lb.(453g) jumbo shrimp, peeled and deveined.
½ yellow onion, chopped.
2 tablespoons garlic, minced.
1 teaspoon seafood-seasoning.
¼ cup green onions, chopped.
1 lime.
4 tablespoons plain fat-free yogurt.
½ cup low-fat cheddar cheese.

Tips: Sprinkle more seafood-seasoning over the whole shrimp before placing it on the top of potato.

1. Preheat oven to 400 °F (204 °C). Lightly grease a baking-sheet with cooking-spray.

2. Cut sweet potato in half and place in a large microwave-safe plate face-down and microwave for 8 minutes.

4. Using a teaspoon, remove all the pulp from the sweet-potato skin (if the sweet-potato is not fully cooked, microwave for an additional 2 minutes).

3. Remove tails from shrimp, leaving four with tails for garnishing. Season with seafood seasoning, chopped garlic, and lime juice.

5. In a large frying pan over medium-high heat, place shrimp and cook for 2 minutes on each side.

Chop the shrimp in small pieces, leaving the four with tails whole for garnishing.

7. Mix potato puree with shrimp pieces (if the puree is too thick add 2 tablespoon of water).Finish with chopped green onion and season with salt and pepper to taste.

8. Fill the potato skin with the puree, sprinkle the cheese on top and bake for five minutes. Before serving, garnish each skin with one of the whole shrimp you set aside and top with fat-free yogurt.

Calories	Protein	Carbs	sugar	Total Fat	Sat Fat	Fiber
239	22g	16g	5g	5g	1g	3g

STUFFED PUMPKIN
WITH SHRIMP STEW

Total time: 30 min.
Prep: 15 min.
Cook: 15 min.
Yield: 4 portions.

Ingredients:

2 lbs. (907 g) peeled, deveined
uncooked jumbo shrimp.
1 medium whole pumpkin.
2 cups all-natural pumpkin purée.
1 cup light coconut milk.
½ cup low-fat mozzarella cheese.
½ cup cilantro, chopped.
2 garlic cloves, minced.
Juice of 1 lime (2 tablespoons).
1 large green bell pepper, chopped.
2 teaspoons Cajun seasoning.
½ teaspoon salt.
1 tablespoon olive oil.

1. Wash pumpkin; with the tip of a
sharp knife cut a circle around
top stem as shown in the photo.

3. In a large bowl, place peeled
shrimp (Leaving 4 with tail on
for garnishing), lime juice,
minced garlic, half of the
chopped cilantro, olive oil, salt
and pepper. Mix well and let
marinate while pumpkin cooks
in microwave.

2. Remove seeds and loose fibers from
inside using a spoon as shown in the
photo. Place pumpkin in a large
microwave-safe plate, pour ½ cup
water inside the pumpkin and
microwave for 8 minutes.

4. Once pumpkin is cooked,
carefully hold using a cloth.
(to prevent burning your
fingers) and remove as
much of the cooked pulp as
you can with a spoon as
shown in the photo. Set
aside.

5. Preheat a nonstick large frying pan
over medium-high heat, add seasoned
marinated shrimps and let it cook for
2 minutes stirring occasionally.

6. Take out 4 shrimps and reserve
for garnishing at the end.

7. In the same frying pan place 2 cups of pumpkin
puree, cooked pumpkin pulp you set aside,
mozzarella, chopped cilantro, chopped bell
pepper and Cajun seasoning to cooked shrimp
and stir well until you have a nice creamy sauce.
Stuff pumpkin with the creamy stew, garnish
with reserved shrimp. Serve right away.

Calories	Protein	Carbs	sugar	Total Fat	Sat Fat	Fiber
397	46g	22g	1g	12g	5g	5g

SARDINE TART
WITH ROASTED PEPPERS AND BLACK OLIVES

Total time: 35 min.
Prep: 10 min.
Cook: 25 min.
Yield: 8 servings.

Ingredients:

For the base:

2 cups gluten-free all-purpose flour.
2 cups unsweetened almond milk.
2 large eggs.
1 tablespoon extra-virgin olive oil.
2 teaspoons baking-powder.
1 teaspoon salt.
1 tablespoon onion powder.

For the topping:

1 cup broccoli, chopped.
1 cup low-fat Mozzarella.
2 cans sardines in olive oil (drained).
2 fire roasted red peppers, sliced.
1 tablespoon tomato paste.
3 tablespoons water.
½ red onion, sliced.
15 pitted black olives to decorate.

1. Preheat oven to 400 °F (204 °C). Spray a 15″ baking-sheet with baking-spray.

2.

In a large bowl, mix eggs and milk until well-combined, then add the flour, olive oil, salt, onion powder and baking-powder mix until the mixture has no lumps.

4.

Pour the batter onto the greased baking-sheet and bake it for 20 minutes.

3.

Add the chopped broccoli and mix again.

5.

To make sure that the tart is fully cooked, insert a toothpick into the center of the cake; if is fully baked it will come out dry. If it is not fully baked return the baking-sheet to the oven for an additional 5 minutes.

6.

Dilute the tomato paste into the 3 tablespoons of water and mix well. Spread the tomato sauce on the tart followed by the cheese.

7.

Top with the remaining ingredients and bake it for another 5 minutes

Calories	Protein	Carbs	sugar	Total Fat	Sat Fat	Fiber
257	15g	25g	2g	10g	1g	5g

CRAB STUFFED EGGPLANT

Total time: 35 min
Prep: 10 min
Cook: 25 min
Yield: 4 servings

Ingredients:

2 large eggplants, cut in half lengthwise.
2 large tomatoes, diced.
½ red onion, chopped.
2 garlic cloves, minced.
2 cans crab meat, drained.
½ cup low-fat grated mozzarella cheese.
½ teaspoon Cajun seasoning.
¼ cup parsley, chopped.
¼ teaspoon salt.

1. Preheat oven to 390 °F (198 °C). Lightly grease baking-pan with cooking-spray.

2. Cut eggplants in half lengthwise. With the tip of a knife, cut around the inside edge to separate the pulp and scoop out the center, leaving enough pulp attached to skin so it will hold the filling and the shape when baked. Set removed pulp aside.

4. Chop tomatoes, red onion and dice garlic. Cut scooped-eggplant pulp in small cubes, chop parsley finely and set aside.

3. On a large plate, add cold water and a pinch of salt and place halved eggplant face down as shown in the photo (this will prevent eggplant from discoloring and also remove the bitter taste).

5. In a frying pan at medium-high heat, place chopped onions and stir fry for 2 minutes.

6. then add chopped tomatoes, eggplant cubes, drained crabmeat, Cajun seasoning, salt, and chopped parsley and let it cook for 2 minutes.

7. Fill each half of eggplant with the stuffing and finish up with grated cheese. Bake for 20-25 minutes.

Calories	Protein	Carbs	sugar	Total Fat	Sat Fat	Fiber
138	13g	18g	7g	0.9g	0.3g	9g

ATLANTIC SALMON CEVICHE

Total time: 15 min.
Prep time: 10 min.
Cook: 5 min.
Yield: 4 servings.

Ingredients:

12 ounces (340g) fresh Atlantic salmon.
2 medium avocados.
2 limes.
2 tablespoons cilantro, chopped.
½ red onion, finely sliced.
5 grape or cherry tomatoes, halved.
1 tablespoon extra-virgin olive oil.
½ teaspoon salt.
¼ teaspoon black pepper.

1.

Cut salmon into 1 x 1-inches (2.5 cm) cubes.

2.

Slice red onion finely.

3.

Slice tomatoes for garnishing and set aside.

4.

Cut avocado in half, remove the seed and slide lemon around the edges of avocado to prevent it from oxidizing and discoloring.

5.

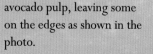

With a teaspoon, scoop out avocado pulp, leaving some on the edges as shown in the photo.

6.

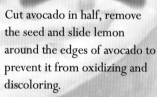

Slice avocados in small cubes.

7.

In a medium, bowl place salmon cubes, sliced avocado, sliced onion, chopped cilantro, freshly squeezed lime juice, olive oil, and salt and pepper. Gently toss, then put mixture back into avocado-shells and top with sliced tomatoes. Serve cold.

Calories	Protein	Carbs	sugar	Total Fat	Sat Fat	Fiber
339	19g	10g	1g	23g	4g	1g

MEDITERRANEAN COUSCOUS

Total time: 30 min.
Pep: 20 min.
Cook: 10 min.
Yield: 6 slices.

Ingredients:

2 cups uncooked couscous.
2 and ½ cups boiling water.
½ red onion, chopped.
2 garlic cloves, minced.
1 large tomato, chopped.
1 lbs. (453g) cooked shrimp.
½ cup frozen green peas.
1 tablespoon tomato paste.
¼ cup parsley, chopped.
1 and ½ teaspoon seasoned salt.
½ cup chopped hearts of palm (optional).
½ cup chopped green olives with peppers.
2 cans sardines in extra-virgin olive oil, drained.
3 large boiled eggs.
½ jar roasted bell pepper sliced (Optional).

1. Cook 3 eggs in boiling water for 10 minutes. Peel, slice and set aside.

2.

In a large pan over medium-high heat, stir-fry chopped onion, minced garlic, chopped tomato, then add shrimp. Let it cook for 2 minutes while mixing well.

4.

Couscous texture should be moist as shown in the photo so there is no need to cover the cooking pan while cooking.

3.

In the same pan, add boiling water, tomato paste, green peas, seasoned salt and chopped parsley to the mixture, then add couscous. Let simmer for another 2 minutes, then turn off heat.

5.

Start decorating the couscous by placing the cooked mixture in a baking-pan. First place a layer of sliced eggs, chopped green olives, slices of roasted bell pepper on the edges as shown in the photo, then add chopped hearts of palm and sardines (previously drained).

6.

Continue building the layers by successively adding cooked couscous, sliced eggs, hearts of palm, sardines, olives, and bell peppers.

7.

Finish the layers with the remaining couscous and press down firmly but carefully in order to compact the mixture by using a spoon to form the desired shape. Demold over a large plate and serve right away.

Calories	Protein	Carbs	sugar	Total Fat	Sat Fat	Fiber
458	33g	54g	6g	11g	2g	4g

SALMON SPREAD

Total time: 30 min.
Prep: 10 min.
Cook: 20 min.
Yield: 4 portions.

Ingredients:

1 lb. (453 g) boneless, skinless fresh salmon.
Juice of 1 large lime.
4 egg whites, boiled.
⅔ cup low-fat cream cheese.
¼ cup fresh parsley, chopped.
¼ cup fresh chives, chopped.
½ red onion, chopped.
¼ cup capers, chopped.
1 teaspoon dry dill (optional).
Salt and pepper to taste.

1. Preheat oven to 390 °F (198 °C) and lightly grease baking-pan with cooking-spray and, in a small pan, cook eggs in warm water for 10 minutes.

2.

Season salmon with ½ teaspoon salt and ½ teaspoon pepper. Bake for 15 minutes. While salmon is in the oven, start chopping red onions, parsley, chives, and capers finely. Set aside.

4.

Peel eggs, cut in half and remove yolks then chop egg whites in small pieces. You may use the egg yolks for anything else but they are not needed for this recipe.

3.

Remove salmon from oven and over a plate using two forks start breaking it into small pieces.

5.

In a large bowl, place shredded salmon, chopped egg whites, cream cheese, chopped onion, chopped parsley, chopped chives, chopped capers, lime juice and adjust the salt to taste by adding a pinch if needed. Remember capers are already salty so take that into account when adjusting salt.

6.

You should end up with a creamy mixture almost like a pâté. Keep refrigerated and serve cold over crackers. This spread should keep for about 2 days if properly refrigerated. Serve with whole wheat/grain crackers.

Tips: You can also use this spread to make some salmon and watercress sandwiches using whole wheat bread.

Calories	Protein	Carbs	sugar	Total Fat	Sat Fat	Fiber
261	34g	9g	6g	13g	2g	0.6g

Calories without crackers.

CRAB CAKE
WITH CREAMY PICO DE GALLO

Total time: 35 min.
Prep: 15 min.
Cook: 20 min.
Yield: 6 crab cakes.

Ingredients:

1 lb. (453g) crabmeat, drained.
6 mini sweet peppers, chopped.
¼ cup parsley, chopped.
1 large egg.
1 red onion, diced.
½ teaspoon salt.
½ teaspoon lemon pepper.
½ cup breadcrumbs

For creamy Pico de Gallo:

1 tablespoon Dijon mustard.
2 tablespoons extra-virgin olive oil.
Juice of one lime.
1 tomato diced small.
2 Serrano peppers.
¼ cup chopped cilantro.
Salt and pepper to taste.

1. Preheat oven to 400 °F (208 °C). Lightly grease a baking-pan big enough to fit 6 cakes.

2.

Chop tomato in small cubes, remove top and stem from Serrano peppers (leaving some stem if you want your salsa a little spicy). Dice peppers finely and chop cilantro.

4.

With a sharp knife, remove the top of sweet peppers and the entire stem and chop finely. Chop red onion and parsley also very finely.

3.

In a small bowl, mix together chopped tomato, diced Serrano pepper, chopped cilantro, lemon juice, Dijon mustard, olive oil and remaining half chopped onion and finish with salt and pepper. Mix well and serve cold on top of crab cakes.

5.

In a medium bowl, place drained crabmeat, chopped peppers, parsley, half of the chopped onion, egg, salt and lemon pepper. Mix well until all ingredients are well-combined.

6.

Cut small pieces of aluminum foil or plastic wrap and add 2 tablespoon into a cookie-cutter and press down the spoon to from the cakes (Alternatively, you may shape the cakes using the palm of your hand).

7.

Preheat a nonstick frying pan lightly greased with cooking-spay and cook crab cakes for 2 minutes per side or until you see significant browning. Transfer browned crab cakes to baking tray and bake in oven for 10 minutes. Serve with a green salad.

Calories	Protein	Carbs	sugar	Total Fat	Sat Fat	Fiber
155	14g	10g	2g	5g	0.8g	1g

BRAZILIAN TILAPIA STEW

Total time: 30 min.
Prep: 15 min.
Cook: 15 min.
Yield: 4 portions.

Ingredients:

2 lbs. (907 g) fresh tilapia filet.
1 large yellow onion, sliced.
Juice of 1 large lime.
Juice of 1 large lemon.
1 orange, juiced.
3 garlic cloves, minced.
1 teaspoon salt.
½ teaspoon pepper.
1 tablespoon extra-virgin olive oil.
4 tomatoes, sliced.
3 bell peppers, diced (1 red, 1 yellow & 1 red).
2 tablespoons tomato paste.
1 teaspoon hot sauce.
½ cup cilantro, chopped.
½ cup parsley, chopped.
1 and ½ cups light coconut milk.

1.

In a large plate, lay tilapia filets, season with salt and pepper and add minced garlic, lime, lemon and orange juices. Add olive oil, turn fillets to coat with marinade and let sit for 10 minutes.

3.

Cut bell peppers in halves, remove tops and stems and then chop into small cubes.

2.

Slice tomatoes and onions as shown in the photo.

4.

Dilute tomato paste with 2 tablespoon of water, add hot sauce and mix well.

5.

To start building, take a large cooking pan and spray with cooking spray (if you have a tagine or clay cooking pan even better), heat to medium-high. Add half of marinated fillets (don't discard the juices) spread tomato sauce evenly over fillets.

6.

Continue building by laying down slices of tomato, onion, chopped peppers, capers, cilantro and parsley, then add coconut milk. Finish up adding the other half of fillets and the marinade juices. Cover cooking pan and cook for 15 minutes.

TIPS: Add 1 lb. (453g) Shrimp to stew between layers and serve with quick potatoes. (see Sides section for recipes) *Adding shrimp Calories will increase 96 calories per portion.*

Calories	Protein	Carbs	sugar	Total Fat	Sat Fat	Fiber
298	25g	22g	13g	12g	5g	4g

SIDES

BAKED ONION BLOSSOM
WITH CHIPOTLE YOGURT DIP

Total time: 25 min.
Prep: 10 min.
Cook: 15 min.
Yield: 4 servings.

Ingredients:

3 medium white onions.
1 whole egg.
⅓ cup 2% low-fat milk or almond milk.
¼ cup gluten-free all-purpose flour.
2 tablespoons coconut flour.
½ teaspoon paprika.
1 teaspoon baking powder.
1 cup breadcrumbs.
½ teaspoon salt.

For the chipotle yogurt dip:

1 (5oz) container plain fat-free yogurt.
2 tablespoons chipotle sauce.
½ teaspoon dry parsley.
Salt and pepper to taste.

1. Preheat oven to 400 °F (218 °C). Lightly grease a baking-pan with cooking-spray.

2.

Peel onions and cut in 4 wedges.

4.

Insert toothpick in each wedge as shown in the picture to prevent wedges from separating.

3.

Cut each wedge in 2. Carefully place wedges on a microwave safe plate and pre-cook for 1 minute.

5.

Mix egg, milk, flours, paprika, baking-powder, and salt. Dip the wedges one by one making sure they're fully coated with the batter and let excess batter drip.

6.

Place wedges into the bread crumb mixture and gently press crumbs into wedges.

7.

Place wedges in prepared baking-pan and bake it for 15 minutes or until golden brown.

8.

For the dip sauce; simply combine yogurt, chipotle, parsley, salt and pepper to taste. Mix well and serve cold.

Calories	Protein	Carbs	sugar	Total Fat	Sat Fat	Fiber
206	13g	39g	13g	2g	0.6g	6g

CARROT BATONS

Total time: 15 min.
Prep: 10 min.
Cook: 5 min.
Yield: 3 sides.

Ingredients:

3 large carrots, peeled.
1 tablespoon extra-virgin olive oil.
1 tablespoon garlic, diced.
1 tablespoon fine herbs.
½ teaspoon kosher salt.
Pepper to taste.

1.

Wash and peel carrots. (If using Organic carrots there is no need to peel)

3.

Slice carrots lengthwise into 4 strips.

5.

Place carrots into a microwave-safe plate with 1 tablespoon of water and microwave for 2 minutes.

2.

Remove stem and cut carrots in half.

4.

Cut each strip into 3 batons as seem in the picture.

6.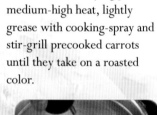

Heat a nonstick frying pan over medium-high heat, lightly grease with cooking-spray and stir-grill precooked carrots until they take on a roasted color.

7.

Place carrots into a bowl, add fine herbs, diced garlic, salt, pepper, and finish with the extra-virgin olive oil. Toss and serve.

Calories	Protein	Carbs	sugar	Total Fat	Sat Fat	Fiber
101	1.4g	13g	5g	5g	0.7g	5g

AUBERGINE CARPACCIO

Total time: 25 min.
Prep: 10 min.
Cook: 15 min.
Yield: 2 servings.

Ingredients:

1 large eggplant, sliced crosswise.
1 tablespoon extra-virgin olive oil.
⅓ cup cilantro, chopped.
2 garlic-cloves, minced.
1 large tomato, seeds removed.
¼ teaspoon cumin.
Salt and pepper to taste.

1. Preheat grill or a nonstick frying pan to medium-high heat.

2. Trim the ends and slice the eggplant into very thin, round pieces, about 2.5 mm. (0.25cm)

4. Arrange the grilled slices on a plate any way you prefer.

3. Place the slices of eggplant onto a grill or frying pan sprayed with cooking-spray and grill them for 1 minute on each side.

5. Slice the tomato into wedges. Remove the seeds by placing the tip of a knife between the pulp and seeds, slicing from one end to the other, removing all the seeds.

6. Finely chop the tomato, garlic and the cilantro.

7. Mix garlic, cilantro and cumin with the olive oil.

8. Drizzle the sauce over the grilled eggplant just before serving and season with salt, pepper. To finish, top he eggplants with the chopped tomatoes.

Calories	Protein	Carbs	sugar	Total Fat	Sat Fat	Fiber
145	3.7g	14g	6g	7g	1g	10g

CURRIED COUSCOUS

Total time: 15 min.
Prep: 5 min.
Cook: 10.
Yield: 4 servings.

Ingredients:

1 cup plain, uncooked couscous.
1 cup water.
½ teaspoon yellow curry powder.
1 large carrot, grated.
¼ cup cilantro, chopped.
½ cup frozen green peas.
½ yellow onion, chopped.
½ teaspoon all-purpose seasoning.
2 garlic cloves, minced.

Tip: You can substitute the yellow curry with turmeric.

1.

Peel and grate carrot and chop onion into small pieces.

3.

Add water to the saucepan and immediately add green peas and chopped cilantro and bring to a boil.

2.

In a medium saucepan greased with cooking-spray, cook grated carrots and chopped onion for 1 minute over medium-high heat.

4.

Add couscous to boiling water.

5.

Stir quickly to separate and mix everything.

6.

Remove saucepan from heat, cover and let stand for 2 minutes.

7.

Uncover saucepan and using a fork separate and fluff couscous Serve immediately.

Calories	Protein	Carbs	sugar	Total Fat	Sat Fat	Fiber
195	7g	39g	3g	1g	0g	3g

BROWN RICE QUICHE

Total time: 40 min.
Prep: 15 min.
Cook: 25 min.
Yield: 6 servings.

Ingredients:

For the base:

5 cups cooked brown rice.
1 large egg.
¾ cup fat free cream cheese.
½ teaspoon all purpose seasoning.

For the filling:

2 and ½ cups low-fat 2% cottage cheese.
2 whole eggs.
1 cup carrot, shredded.
1 cup broccoli, chopped.
⅓ cup parsley, chopped.
1 cup leek, sliced.
1 and ½ tablespoons herbes de Provence.
½ teaspoon salt.
½ teaspoon pepper.
3 large tomatoes.

1. Preheat oven to 375 °F (190 °C). Lightly grease a 9″ (22 cm) fluted tart-pan with cooking-spray.

2.

In a large bowl, mix cooked rice, cream cheese, egg, salt, and herbs. Mix until very well-combined. (Place cream cheese in microwave for 10 seconds to soften up)

3.

Fill pre-greased tart-pan with the rice mixture, pressing rice onto the bottom and up the sides to form a crust as shown in the photo.

4.

In a medium bowl mix cottage cheese, eggs, shredded carrot, chopped broccoli, chopped parsley, sliced leek, herbes de Provence, and salt and pepper. Set aside.

5.

Cut tomato in half, then slice into 8 wedges as shown in the photo and gently season with salt and pepper to taste.

6.

Place mixture on top of the rice crust in the baking pan, garnish with sliced tomatoes around the quiche as shown in the photo and bake in the middle oven rack for 20-25 minutes, or until top is browned.

Tip: This side is a complete meal if you eat 1 and ½ portions.

Calories	Protein	Carbs	sugar	Total Fat	Sat Fat	Fiber
376	24g	51g	9g	6g	1g	3g

QUICK & EASY POTATOES

Total time: 15 min.
Prep: 5 min.
Cook: 10 min.
Yield: 4 servings.

Ingredients:

1 lb. (453 g) baby red potatoes.
½ teaspoon salt.
½ teaspoon paprika.
½ teaspoon garlic powder.
2 tablespoons parsley, chopped.
1 tablespoon extra virgin olive oil.

Tip: If you can't find baby red potatoes use another smooth skin potato such as Yukon gold.

1.

Cut potatoes in half. In a microwave safe large bowl add potatoes, ½ cup water and microwave for 4-5 minutes. Insert a tip of knife to make sure it is cooked, if comes out easily it is cooked.

3.

Cook potatoes for 2-3 minutes or until you see significant browning.

2.

Over medium-high setting heat a non-stick frying pan, coat lightly with cooking spray and then add the precooked potatoes faced down.

4.

Mix all the ingredients for the seasoning, place Potatoes in a bowl and sprinkle seasoning mix over potatoes. Finish up with a drizzle of olive oil. Mix and serve.

Calories	Protein	Carbs	sugar	Total Fat	Sat Fat	Fiber
123	3g	21g	0.8g	3g	0.3g	3g

CRUNCHY PICKLES

Total time: 25 min.
Prep: 10 min.
Cook: 15 min.
Yield: 4 portions.

Ingredients:

1O large whole dill pickles.
¾ cup bread crumbs (Whole-wheat preferable).
⅓ cup yellow corn-meal.
2 teaspoons baking-powder.
1 teaspoon garlic salt.
2 teaspoons turmeric.
2 tablespoons dry parsley.
1 large egg.

For the dip:

1 cup 2% low-fat cottage cheese.
1 teaspoon ranch seasoning powder.

1. Preheat oven to 400 °F (204 °C) lightly grease a baking-dish with cooking-spray.

2.

Wash pickles to remove excess sodium, drain and pat dry with a paper towel.

3.

Cut pickle in half, then in half again forming 4 wedge-shaped batons.

4.

Place pickles in a bowl and add the egg. Mix well until all pickles are coated with egg.

5.

In a large plate, mix bread crumbs, corn meal, baking-powder, garlic salt, turmeric, and dry parsley with a fork until well-combined.

6.

Add the pickles to the flour mixture until well-coated.

7.

Bake for 15 minutes. For the cottage cheese dip, combine cheese and ranch seasoning, mix well and serve cold.

Calories	Protein	Carbs	sugar	Total Fat	Sat Fat	Fiber
205	10g	31g	5g	3g	0.8g	5g

YUMMY YAMS

Total time: 10 min.

Prep: 2 min.

Cook: 8 min.

Yield: 3 portions.

Ingredients:

3 medium yams (sweet potatoes) 5 oz. Each. (141 g).halved.

1 tablespoon salt-free seasoning.

1 tablespoon reduced-fat Parmesan cheese.

2 tablespoons parsley, chopped.

½ tablespoon extra-virgin olive oil.

Tip: you may keep this dish refrigerated for 2 days. To warm up, just microwave for 1 minute.

1. Run yams under water and gently clean to remove any dirt.

Cut yams in half.

4.

Finely chop parsley. Set aside.

3.

In a microwave-safe plate, pour ¼ cup water and lay down potatoes face down as shown in photo. Microwave 4-5 minutes. To make sure yams are completely cooked, insert a fork in the middle of yams; if comes out easily it is cooked.

5.

Mix Parmesan cheese with salt-free seasoning.

6.

Preheat a nonstick frying pan, lightly greased with cooking-spray, over medium-high heat and place cooked yams face down. Let cook for 1-2 minutes or until you see significant browning as shown in photo.

7.

Drizzle extra-virgin olive oil over yams, then seasoning and finish up with chopped parsley on top. Serve right away.

Calories	Protein	Carbs	sugar	Total Fat	Sat Fat	Fiber
143	3g	26g	5g	3g	0.8g	5g

SPICY POTATO WEDGES

Total time: 30 min.
Prep: 5 min.
Cook: 25 min.
Yield: 4 portions.

Ingredients:

4 large pink potatoes or Russet potatoes.
2 teaspoons paprika.
½ teaspoon cayenne pepper.
1 teaspoon seasoned salt.
½ teaspoon garlic powder.
½ tablespoon extra-virgin olive oil

1. Preheat oven to 500 °F (260 °C). Prepare a large baking-sheet, lining with wax paper or aluminum foil, and lightly spray cooking-spray.

2.

Cut potatoes in half, then in half again until you have 4 wedges.

4.

Place washed potatoes over a kitchen paper towel and thoroughly pat dry. This will help potato crispiness.

3.

In a large bowl filled with water, place potato wedges and stir them with your hands. This will remove the starch from wedges and prevent them from sticking to each other.

5.

In a large bowl, place potato wedges then add olive oil, paprika, cayenne pepper, seasoned salt and garlic powder. Mix well with your hands, ensuring that all wedges are coated as shown in the photo.

6.

Place potatoes over prepared baking-pan and bake for a total of 25 minutes. About hallway to 15 minutes into baking time, flip the wedges to ensure all sides are crisped. You may set your oven to "broil" for 2 minutes at the end for better crispiness if necessary. If you have silicone baking mat I strongly recommend using it for this recipe instead of wax paper or aluminum foil.

Calories	Protein	Carbs	sugar	Total Fat	Sat Fat	Fiber
151	4g	29g	1g	2g	0.1g	3g

119

GARLIC CAULIFLOWER PURÉE

Total time: 15 min.
Cook: 8 min.
Prep: 7 min.
Yield: 2 portions.

Ingredients:

1 medium cauliflower head.
2 garlic cloves.
1 tablespoon extra-virgin olive oil.
½ teaspoon salt.
½ teaspoon pepper.
1 tablespoon Dijon mustard.
2 rashers lean turkey-bacon.
¼ cup reduced fat cheddar cheese, grated.
¼ cup green onion, chopped.

1.

With the tip of a knife, separate cauliflower into florets and cut into small pieces.

2.

Place cauliflower pieces into a large microwave-safe bowl with 2 garlic cloves and ¼ cup water, cook for 4 minutes.

3.

In a blender, blend cooked cauliflower, olive oil, garlic cloves, Dijon mustard, salt and pepper for approx. 2 minutes until smooth. The resulting consistency must be creamy and not watery. If mixture is too thick, slowly add water as needed in 1 tablespoon increments.

4.

In a microwave-safe dish, lay down 2 sheets of paper towels, place the bacon rashers and microwave for 1 and ½ minutes or until crispy. Chop in small pieces and set aside.

5.

Pour cauliflower purée into a serving-dish and top with grated cheddar cheese, chopped green onion and chopped turkey-bacon.

Calories	Protein	Carbs	sugar	Total Fat	Sat Fat	Fiber
211	12g	16g	6g	11g	2g	6g

UNFRIED FRENCH FRIES

Total time: 35 min.
Prep: 5 min.
Cook: 30 min.
Yield: 4 portions.

Ingredients:

2 larges russet potatoes. Approx.
10 oz. each (290 g)
1 tablespoon, extra virgin olive oil.
½ teaspoon, seasoned salt.
1 teaspoon, dry parsley (Optional)

Tip: You can add ½ teaspoon cayenne
pepper for spicy fries or ½ teaspoon of
truffle oil before serving (truffle oil
will increase overall calories)

1. Preheat oven to 500 °F (260 °C). Line a baking pan with wax paper or
aluminum foil, and generously spray with cooking spray.

2.

Cut potatoes into wedges
then into strips.

3.

In a large bowl filled with water
add potato strips, and then wash
them.

6.

Lay down potatoes over prepared
baking pan, and then bake for 30
minutes. There is no need to turn
potatoes and sometimes they stick
to the wax paper (it is normal)
after 30 minutes it will come out
just fine. If you have silicone baking
mat I strongly recommend using it
for this recipe instead of wax paper
or aluminum foil.

4.

Drain and lay down potatoes over
paper towel and pat making sure
all strips are dry.

5.

In a large bowl add potatoes, olive
oil, seasoned salt, and dry parsley,
mix well until all strips are coated
with the olive oil.

Calories	Protein	Carbs	sugar	Total Fat	Sat Fat	Fiber
169	4g	29g	2g	4g	0.3g	3g

MEXICAN QUINOA

Total time: 25 min.
Prep: 10 min.
Cook: 15 min.
Yield: 4 portions.

Ingredients:

1 cup cooked black beans, drained.
1 cup uncooked quinoa.
2 and ½ cups boiling water.
1 red bell pepper, chopped.
1 yellow pepper, chopped.
1 red onion, chopped.
2 garlic cloves, minced.
4 green tomatillos, sliced.
1 cup corn kernels.
1 jalapeño, minced.
1 large avocado, diced.
1 tablespoon extra-virgin olive oil.
1 teaspoon seasoned salt.
½ teaspoon pepper.
½ teaspoon cumin.
½ teaspoon paprika.
½ cup fresh cilantro, chopped.

1.

Chop peppers, jalapeño, onion, and mince garlic.

3.

Slice tomatillos into wedges, and chop cilantro leaves.

5.

Add quinoa, beans, corn, boiling water, salt, pepper, cumin, paprika and mix well. Cover and cook for 10-15 minutes. If quinoa is not cooked after 15 minutes add more water and cook for an additional 5 minutes or so.

2.

Heat a large frying pan over medium-high heat, spray with cooking-spray, then add chopped onion and minced garlic. Let it cook for 1 minute, then add chopped peppers and jalapeño, stir and cook for 1 more minute.

4.

In a medium bowl, mix sliced tomatillos with salt and pepper to taste, finishing with 1 tablespoon olive oil. Mix well and set aside.

6.

Peel avocado and chop into small cubes. Top cooked quinoa with avocado mix well.

7.

Decorate with tomatillo wedges and chopped cilantro. Serve immediately.

Calories	Protein	Carbs	sugar	Total Fat	Sat Fat	Fiber
226	8g	30g	4g	8g	1g	9g

BREAKFAST

ONE-PAN EGGS & PEPPERS

TURKISH BREAKFAST

Total time: 25 min.
Prep: 10 min.
Cook: 15 min.
Yield: 3 servings.

Ingredients:

3 whole eggs.
3 egg whites.
10 oz. (283g) sliced 98% fat-free smoked turkey.
1 red pepper, chopped.
1 yellow bell pepper, sliced.
1 green bell pepper, sliced.
3 large tomatoes, sliced.
1 medium red onion, sliced.
1 Poblano chili, chopped (optional).

For parsley garlic yogurt dressing:

1 and ½ cups fat-free Greek yogurt.
1 tablespoon extra-virgin olive oil.
2 tablespoons parsley, finely chopped.
1 teaspoon garlic, minced.
Salt and pepper to taste.

1.

In a small bowl, combine minced garlic, yogurt, parsley, olive oil, salt, and pepper. Mix well.

2.

Chop smoked turkey into fine strips. Set aside.

5.

Crack 1 egg into a small bowl or cup and add one egg white for each whole egg. You will need to repeat this operation 3 times (one for each pocket).

3.

Cut bell peppers in half, removing top and stem, then slice thinly. Do the same with onion, tomato and Poblano peppers, removing seeds if you prefer less spicy.

4.

Heat frying pan over medium-high heat and spray with cooking-spay, then place onions, peppers, tomato and chili and cook for about 3 minutes until they begin to soften. Add chopped turkey and cook for and additional 2minutes.

6.

Using a spoon, create 3 pockets and add one whole egg and one egg white in each pocket. Cover the pan and cook the eggs over a low heat until just set (about 5 minutes). Drizzle with extra-virgin olive oil and sprinkle chopped parsley. Serve on the pan with yogurt dressing and toasted whole wheat bread.

Calories	Protein	Carbs	sugar	Total Fat	Sat Fat	Fiber
384	36g	22g	9g	10g	1g	4g

Without the bread.

129

BREAKFAST POCKETS

Total time: 30 min.
Prep: 15 min.
Cook: 15 min.
Yield: 4 Portions.

Ingredients:

5 eggs.
4 whole-grain baguettes.
½ cup red onion, chopped.
½ cup grape tomatoes.
½ cup low-fat Mexican four
cheese, grated.
1 large Portobello mushroom,
chopped.
10 oz. (283g) cooked chicken
breast, diced.
1 handful spinach, chopped.
1 tablespoon yellow mustard.
2 tablespoons cilantro, chopped.
Salt and pepper to taste.

1. Preheat oven to 390° F (198° C).

2. Cut bread in half lengthwise.

4. Chop Portobello, cooked chicken breast, spinach, red onions and grape tomatoes. Set Aside.

3. Using your fingers, remove excess bread from both halves, leaving shells.

5. Over medium-high heat, add onions, tomato and chicken. Stir-fry for 2 minutes

6. In a large bowl, mix the chopped ingredients with the grated cheese and season with salt and pepper.

7. Fill the pockets with this mixture, leaving a space/hole for the egg.

8. Carefully crack egg into the space/hole and bake the pockets for 15 minutes or until eggs are cooked to your liking.

Calories	Protein	Carbs	sugar	Total Fat	Sat Fat	Fiber
357	39g	34g	3g	7g	2g	4g

BREAKFAST MUFFINS

Total time: 30 min.
Prep: 10 min.
Cook: 20 min.
Yield: 8 Muffins.

Ingredients:

½ cup almond milk (unsweetened).
3 large eggs.
½ cup rye flour.
1 tablespoon flax seed (optional).
½ teaspoon salt.
½ teaspoon black pepper.
1 teaspoon paprika.
½ tablespoon herbes de Provence.
1 teaspoon baking-powder.
½ cup broccoli, chopped.
¼ cup red onion, chopped.
½ cup carrot, shredded.
2 tablespoons parsley, chopped.
½ cup ham (95% fat free), diced.
½ cup low-fat mozzarella cheese.

1. Preheat oven to 400 °F (204 °C). Coat muffin pan evenly with nonstick cooking-spray.

2.

Shred the carrot and chop the onion, broccoli and parsley. Set aside.

3.

In a large bowl, beat milk and eggs using a whisk or fork.

4.

Add the flour, flax seed, salt, pepper, paprika, herbes de Provence, and baking-powder. Mix well.

5.

Combine the mixture with chopped vegetables.

6.

Using a tablespoon fill the muffin cavities with the batter.

7.

Top with shredded cheese and bake for 20 minutes.

Calories	Protein	Carbs	sugar	Total Fat	Sat Fat	Fiber
115	9g	8g	2g	5g	2g	2g

ITALIAN BREAD

Total time: 45 min.
Cook: 25 min.
Prep: 20 min.
Yield: 6 slices.

Ingredients:

3 cups gluten free pizza crust mix.
½ cup additional gluten free pizza crust mix (for kneading).
2 tablespoons dry yeast.
2 tablespoons dry oregano.
2 tablespoons garlic powder.
1 cup warm water.
¼ cup extra-virgin olive oil.
1 tablespoon brown sugar.
1 large egg.
1 teaspoon salt.

For the stuffing:

1 cup fresh baby spinach.
5 slices low-fat turkey bacon.
10 slices lean turkey deli meat.
10 slices low-fat mozzarella cheese.
1 red bell pepper, sliced.
½ cup green olives, pitted.
1 tablespoon low-fat Parmesan cheese.
1 teaspoon extra-virgin olive oil.

1. Preheat oven to 425 °F (218 °C). Lightly grease a 12″ (30 cm) flat pan with cooking-spray.

2.

In a large bowl, mix brown sugar, dry yeast, olive oil and warm water (not hot, slightly above body temperature.). Mix all the ingredients until sugar and yeast are dissolved and let the yeast work for 5 minutes. After 5 minutes your should see little bubbles forming which means your yeast is "live" and good to go.

4.

In order to knead the dough without it sticking to your kneading surface (tabletop, wood surface, marble board etc.), you will need to continuously cover your work-surface with a bit of flour while you knead (about ½ cup of flour in total should suffice). Start kneading dough by pressing the heels of your hands into the dough, pushing forward slightly and adding flour little by little.

3.

In the same bowl, add flour, dry oregano, garlic powder, egg, and salt. Using a large spoon, mix well until all ingredients are combined. Resulting dough should be thoroughly wet with no dry spots.

5.

Continue to knead until you end up with a uniform, non-sticky dough as shown in photo.

6.

Using a rolling-pin or a wine bottle, start stretching the dough as flat and as thin you can; don't worry about the shape. Once you have the dough spread out to adequate thickness, start adding the stuffing; first add turkey ham then the turkey bacon, olives, sliced bell pepper, cheese, and spinach (in that order).

7.

Start wrapping the roll tight up to the middle; keep rolling up to the second short end. Patting gently throughout the process. As shown in the photo.

8. Place bread on the prepared flat baking-pan and with a fork, punch small holes to release the air from the bread as it bakes. Bake for 20-25 minutes or until golden brown. After bread is baked, brush olive oil on top and sprinkle Parmesan cheese on top. Serve hot.

Calories	Protein	Carbs	sugar	Total Fat	Sat Fat	Fiber
389	22g	24g	4g	22g	6g	3g

FRITTATA VERDE

Total time: 30 min.
Prep: 10 min.
Cook: 20 min.
Yield: 4 servings.

Ingredients:

4 eggs.
5 egg-whites.
1 cup broccoli, chopped.
1 cup kale, chopped.
½ lb.(226g) asparagus.
3 green tomatillos.
5 oz. (141g) 97% lean ham.
½ red onion, diced.
½ cup low-fat mozzarella cheese.
½ teaspoon salt.
¼ teaspoon pepper.
½ teaspoon paprika.
1 teaspoon garlic powder.
1 teaspoon baking-powder.

TIP: Instead of ham you may use smoked salmon, which works really well with this recipe. Calories may vary.

1. Preheat oven to 390 °F (198 °C). For this recipe you will need an iron skillet or an oven-safe frying pan.

2.

Chop kale, broccoli, half of asparagus (stem part) and dice onion, setting aside the top half of asparagus (spears) for topping in step 8

4.

Slice tomatillos by first cutting in half, then into 6 wedges per side as shown in photo. Season with a drizzle of olive oil, salt and pepper. Set aside.

3.

Finely dice ham. Set aside.

5.

Heat skillet on medium heat, spray nonstick vegetable spray, add onions and ham and let it cook for 1 minute. Add the greens and cook for 1 more minute.

6.

Lightly beat the eggs, adding salt, pepper, paprika, garlic powder and the baking-powder.

7.

Pour this mixture over the greens, sprinkle mozzarella on top and let it cook for 3 minutes. Turn heat off and start decorating with the tomatillos wedges.

8.

Top Frittata with the asparagus spears, put the skillet in the preheated oven and bake for 15 minutes.

Calories	Protein	Carbs	sugar	Total Fat	Sat Fat	Fiber
216	22g	11g	4g	9g	2g	3g

RED VELVET PANCAKES

Total time: 20 min.
Prep: 10 min.
Cook: 10 min.
Yield: 10 pancakes.

Ingredients:

1 cup all-purpose gluten-free flour.
½ cup almond flour.
1 teaspoon organic stevia.
1 and ¼ cups unsweetened vanilla almond milk.
1 large egg.
½ beet, peeled and chopped.
3 and ½ teaspoons baking-powder.
3 tablespoons vanilla whey protein (optional).

For the topping:

1 cup fat-free cream cheese.
2 tablespoons unsweetened almond vanilla milk.
1 teaspoon organic stevia.
1 teaspoon vanilla extract.
½ cup blueberries.
6 cherries.
6 strawberries, sliced.
1 small banana, sliced.
2 tablespoons organic agave.

1. Run beets under water and gently clean to remove any dirt.

2. Cover chopping board with aluminum foil or plastic wrap, hold beet with a fork and peel beet with the tip of a knife.

3. Cut beet in half then in four pieces. Set aside

4. In a blender, place almond milk, egg, flours, stevia, protein powder (optional), chopped beet, and baking-powder. Blend for 2 minutes.

5. Preheat a griddle or nonstick frying pan, lightly greased with cooking-spray, over medium-high heat. Pour approx. ⅓ cup of batter in the griddle/pan straight from blender pitcher or using measuring-cup and cook until small bubbles form and the edges starts to dry.

6. Flip and cook until lightly brown on the other side as shown in photo. Repeat steps 4 & 5 for each pancake until you have no batter left. Remember to grease the pan again for every new pancake to avoid sticking.

7. For the Glaze; mix together cream cheese, almond milk, vanilla extract and stevia. Top pancakes with glaze, fruit and a drizzle of organic agave. Serve hot.

Tip: If you want your glaze a little sweeter just add more agave or substitute with honey, being aware that calories and other nutritional values will increase.

Calories	Protein	Carbs	sugar	Total Fat	Sat Fat	Fiber
157	9g	21g	9g	4g	0.5g	3g

Per pancake with topping

SUPER BOWL BREAKFAST

Total time: 10 min.
Prep: 7 min.
Cook: 3 min.
Yield: 2 servings.

Ingredients:

2 cups unsweetened vanilla almond-milk or low-fat milk.
½ cup oats, quick 1-minute.
½ teaspoon organic stevia.
2 tablespoons vanilla whey protein.
2 tablespoons flaxseed meal.
1 teaspoon poppy seeds.
½ cup strawberries, chopped.
½ cup blueberries.
4 cherries.
⅓ cup sliced almonds.
2 tablespoons organic agave.

Tips: You may use any whey protein flavor and you can substitute agave with honey (It may increase calories).

1.

Wash fruits and pat dry with paper towel, remove leaves from strawberries and slice into 4 wedges.

2.

In a medium saucepan, mix milk, oats, flaxseed meal, stevia, and protein powder.

3.

Bring to a boil over medium-high heat, stirring occasionally for 1-2 minutes or until oats start to thicken.

4.

Pour cooked oats into a bowl, sprinkle poppy seeds on top, and then add fruits and agave. Serve right away.

Calories	Protein	Carbs	sugar	Total Fat	Sat Fat	Fiber
348	18g	44g	23g	11g	1g	8g

"

I THINK THE BEST MEAL IS THE ONE COOKED AT HOME. WITH CARE, LOVE AND SIMPLICITY.

SAUCES & DIPS

RUSTIC TOMATO KETCHUP

Total time: 25 min.
Prep: 10 min.
Cook: 15 min.
Yield: 1.6 cup (26 tablespoons).

Ingredients:

6 large, very ripe tomatoes.
1 small yellow onion.
½ cup water.
⅓ cup apple-cider vinegar.
1 tablespoon onion powder.
2 garlic cloves.
1 teaspoon salt.
½ teaspoon black pepper.
1 tablespoon Dijon mustard.
1 teaspoon liquid smoke.
¼ teaspoon ground cinnamon.
½ teaspoon organic stevia.

Tip: This is a rustic ketchup with small pieces of tomato, if you want you can strain to remove pieces and have a more traditional-looking ketchup.

1.

Cut tomatoes in half, peel onion and garlic and also cut in half.

3.

Turn off heat when you see significant browning (almost burnt color), as shown in the photo. Remove onion and garlic. Set aside.

2.

Preheat a nonstick, ungreased frying pan over medium-high heat and place tomatoes, onions and garlic face-down, as shown in the photo. Let cook for 3 minutes.

4.

Mash tomatoes using a potato masher or fork.

5.

Return onions and garlic to the frying pan and add Dijon, water, vinegar, salt, black pepper, liquid smoke, cinnamon, stevia, and garlic powder. Let it simmer for 5 minutes.

6.

Pour this mixture into a blender and blend until smooth for about 2 minutes.

7.

In a small saucepan, place blended ketchup and let it cook for 5 minutes. Let it cool and pour into a jar. This recipe will keep for 4 days if properly refrigerated

Calories	Protein	Carbs	sugar	Total Fat	Sat Fat	Fiber
9	0.3g	1.8g	1g	0.1g	0g	0.5g

Per tablespoon.

CARROT MAYONNAISE

Total time: 13 min.
Prep: 5 min.
Cook: 8 min.
Yield: 9 oz. jar (18 tablespoons).

Ingredients:

4 medium carrots.
¼ cup unsweetened almond milk.
1 and ½ tablespoons fresh lime juice.
¼ cup extra-virgin olive oil.
1 garlic clove.
½ tablespoon dry oregano.
¾ teaspoon salt.
¼ teaspoon pepper.

1.

Peel carrots and remove the ends (discard ends). If using Organic carrots there is no need to peel.

3.
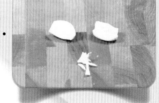
Peel garlic, cut it in half and remove its green center.

2.

Chop carrots and cook in a microwave-safe bowl with 1 tablespoon of water for 4 minutes.

4.

Place cooked carrot, milk, lime juice, olive oil, garlic, oregano, salt and pepper into a blender or food processor, blending until smooth (about 3 minutes).

5.

Keep in the refrigerator. This mayo can keep for up to 4 days in the fridge with proper refrigeration.

Calories	Protein	Carbs	sugar	Total Fat	Sat Fat	Fiber
32	0.1g	1.3g	0.5g	3g	0.5g	0.4g

Per tablespoon.

BLACK OLIVE MAYO

Total time: 7 min.

Prep: 3 min.

Cook: 4 min.

Yield: 12 tablespoons/portions.

Ingredients:

1 whole egg.

1 egg-yolk.

2 tablespoons freshly-squeezed lime juice.

½ cup extra-virgin olive oil.

1 tablespoon Dijon mustard.

½ teaspoon salt.

½ teaspoon pepper.

5 large seedless black olives.

1. Place eggs, lemon juice, extra-virgin olive oil, Dijon, salt and pepper in blender and blend until very creamy (about 3 minutes).

2. Finely dice black olives.

3. Mix diced black olives with blended mayo and put in the refrigerator. This process will make mayo firm and ready to use after it is cold. This mayo will keep for about 4 days in the refrigerator with proper refrigeration.

Raw egg is not recommended for children, elderly, pregnant women, and people with weakened immune systems. Use pasteurized egg yolk instead, to avoid any risk of salmonella infection.

Calories	Protein	Carbs	sugar	Total Fat	Sat Fat	Fiber
94	0.7g	0.4g	0.1g	10g	2g	0.1g

Per tablespoon.

GUACAMOLE

Total time: 15 min.
Prep: 10 min.
Cook: 5 min.
Yield: 2 portions.

Ingredients:

1 large avocado.
1 large tomato, diced.
1 Serrano chili, diced.
½ cup fresh cilantro, chopped.
½ yellow onion, diced.
1 large lime.
1 teaspoon extra-virgin olive oil.
Salt and pepper to taste.

TIPS: 1) If you like your guacamole spicy you can add as much of the Serrano seeds set aside as waste to the mix based on personal preference. 2) Remember the seed in step 4? Although the lime juice should be enough to keep the guacamole from oxidizing and turning black, if you also put the seed inside the mix it will help it keep longer in the fridge with proper refrigeration.

1.

Cut tomato into quarters.

3.

With the tip of a knife, cut Serrano chili lengthwise and remove the middle stem containing the seeds, discard seeds as this is where the "heat" comes from. Finely dice and set aside.

2.

Remove seeds by sliding the tip of the knife to remove flesh and seeds as shown in the photo. Dice into small cubes.

4.

Cut avocado in half, remove the heart/seed and scoop out avocado pulp using a spoon as shown in the photo. Save the avocado seed for a nifty trick.(see tips)

5.

On a large plate, mash avocado with a fork and immediately squeeze juice of a lime on top and mix.

6.
Add diced tomato, diced Serrano, diced onion, chopped cilantro and olive oil, and finish with salt and pepper to taste. Keep refrigerated and serve cold.

Calories	Protein	Carbs	sugar	Total Fat	Sat Fat	Fiber
214	3g	13g	4g	18g	2g	7g

AVOCADO MAYO
WITH BACON BITES

Total time: 10 min.
Prep: 2 min.
Cook: 8 min.
Yield: 8 tablespoons/Portions.

Ingredients:

1 large avocado. (1cup)
Juice of one lime (2 tablespoons).
1 tablespoon Dijon mustard.
⅓ teaspoon salt.
⅓ teaspoon pepper.
¼ cup extra-virgin olive oil.
2 slices lean turkey bacon.
1 tablespoon parsley, chopped.
½ cup filtered water.

TIP: Although the lime juice should be enough to keep the mayo from oxidizing and turning black, if you also put the seed inside the mix it will help it keep longer in the fridge with proper refrigeration.

1.

In a microwave-safe dish, lay down 2 sheets of paper towels, lay the slices of bacon and microwave for 1-2 minutes or until it is crispy.

2.

Cut avocado in half, remove heart/seed and scoop out the pulp with a spoon.

3.

Place avocado pulp, lime juice, Dijon, olive oil, water, salt and pepper in a blender or food processor and blend for 3 minutes.

4.

Chop cooked bacon into small bits.

5.

In a small bowl, mix avocado mayo, chopped parsley and chopped bacon. This recipe should keep for 1 day in the fridge with proper refrigeration.

Calories	Protein	Carbs	sugar	Total Fat	Sat Fat	Fiber
97	1g	2g	0.2g	9g	1g	1g

Per tablespoon.

COLLARD GREENS DIP

Total time: 10 min.
Prep: 5 min.
Cook: 5 min.
Yield: 4 portions.

Ingredients:

1 bunch collard greens, chopped.
2 garlic cloves, minced.
1 (5oz) container fat-free plain Greek yogurt.
1 teaspoon onion powder.
Salt and pepper to taste.

1.

Wash collard greens and pat dry with paper towel. Remove and discard stems as seem in the photo.

3.

Preheat a nonstick frying pan, lightly grease with cooking-spray and cook minced garlic for 30 sec.

2.

Finely slice collard greens.

4.

Add chopped collard greens and cook for 1 minute, mixing well. Turn off heat. You want a very vibrant color for your collard greens so don't let them cook more than 1 minute.

5.

Place cooked collard greens on a chopping-board and chop very finely.

6.

In a medium bowl, combine collard greens, Greek yogurt, onion powder, salt and pepper. Mix well and keep refrigerated. Serve cold. This should keep for 2 days with proper refrigeration.

Calories	Protein	Carbs	sugar	Total Fat	Sat Fat	Fiber
37	5g	4g	1g	0.2g	0g	1g

BBQ SAUCE

Total time: 20 min.
Prep: 5 min.
Cook: 15 min.
Yield: 2 cups, 32 tablespoons.

Ingredients:

3 very ripe romaine tomatoes.
½ yellow onion.
2 tablespoons hickory liquid smoke.
3 garlic cloves.
1 teaspoon apple-cider vinegar.
1 tablespoon organic agave or 1
teaspoon organic stevia.
3 tablespoons Worcestershire sauce.
1 tablespoon yellow mustard.
½ cup chicken-stock or water.
1 teaspoon hot pepper sauce
(optional).
½ teaspoons salt.
½ teaspoon pepper.

1.

Peel garlic and onion and
cut in half.

3.

Preheat a nonstick ungreased frying
pan over medium-high heat and place
tomatoes, onions and garlic face-
down as shown in the photo and let it
cook for 3 minutes to burn a bit.

2.

Cut tomato in half.

4.

When you turn the tomatoes and
see a brown, almost burnt, color
turn the heat off.

5.

Place tomatoes, garlic, onion,
liquid smoke, vinegar, agave or
stevia, Worcestershire sauce,
mustard, chicken stock, hot
sauce, salt and pepper in a
blender and blend for 2
minutes.

6.

Place the blended tomato mix
into a medium-saucepan and
cook over medium-high heat for
10-15 minutes or until it starts
to thicken. This sauce will keep
for 4 days in the fridge with
proper refrigeration.

Calories	Protein	Carbs	sugar	Total Fat	Sat Fat	Fiber
10	0.1g	1g	1g	0.1g	0g	0.2g

Per tablespoon.

KIDS MENU

SPAGHETTI & MEATBALL NESTS

Total time: 40 min.
Prep: 20 min.
Cook: 20 min.
Yield: 12 nests, 6 portions.

Ingredients:

For Meatballs:

1 lb. 93% lean ground beef.
2 cups light tomato sauce.
½ cup carrots, shredded.
1 cup broccoli, finely chopped.
½ teaspoon seasoned salt.
½ yellow onion, chopped.
1 tablespoon yellow mustard.
½ cup black olives, chopped.
2 tablespoons parsley, chopped.
2 tablespoons low fat parmesan cheese. (for topping)

For Meatball Nests:

1 large egg.
½ package whole grain spaghetti.
½ teaspoon salt.
½ cup light tomato sauce.

1. Preheat oven to 400 °F (204 °C). Lightly grease 12-cup nonstick muffin pan with cooking-spray.

2.

Fill a large pot with water and bring to a boil, then cook pasta according to package directions. Drain and set aside.

4.

Pinch enough of the meat mixture and roll between your hands to form small meatballs. Make sure that the meatball will fit on top of your pasta nest (about the diameter of the bottom of a muffin cavity on your pan).

3.

In a large bowl, combine all the ingredients for the meatballs and mix well.

5.

In a bowl, mix the cooked pasta that has cooled to allow handling, with the egg, salt and tomato sauce.

6.

Scoop spaghetti into the cupcake pan, making sure all of the spaghetti fits comfortably inside the cavities and bake it for 15 minutes or until set. Once you have put pasta in the oven proceed to next step.

7.

In a saucepan, heat meatballs and 2 cups tomato sauce over medium-heat until meatballs are heated through (As the meat is very lean, do not pre-sauté the meatballs to avoid them getting dry, cook directly in the tomato sauce). You may use a cover to accelerate the cooking process. Cook for 10 minutes.

Calories	Protein	Carbs	sugar	Total Fat	Sat Fat	Fiber
330	24g	37g	9g	8g	2g	7g

Per 2 nests.

TURKEY QUINOA LOLLIPOPS
WITH YOGURT CILANTRO DIP

Total time: 30 min.
Prep: 15 min.
Cook: 15 min.
Yield: 20 lollipops.

Ingredients:

1 lb. low-fat ground turkey.
1 cup quinoa, cooked.
½ cup sweet mini-peppers, chopped.
½ cup yellow onion, chopped.
1 tablespoon Dijon mustard.
1 tablespoon Worcestershire sauce.
¼ cup parsley, chopped.
1 and ½ teaspoons reduced sodium
seasoned salt.
Bamboo lollipop sticks.

Smoked yogurt cilantro dip:

1 (5oz) container plain fat-free yogurt.
1 tablespoon water.
1 handful fresh cilantro.
1 teaspoon liquid smoke.
Salt and pepper to taste.

1. Preheat oven to 400 °F (204 °C). Lightly grease baking-sheet with cooking-spray.

2.

Cut the pepper in half with a knife, removing the veins and seeds.

3.

Finely chop peppers and onion.

4.

In a large bowl, add ground turkey, quinoa, peppers, onion, mustard, Worcestershire sauce, parsley and seasoned salt.

5.

Combine all ingredients, (first with a spoon, then your clean hands) to mix all ingredients thoroughly.

6.

Grease your hands with cooking-spray and make small, bite-size meatballs by using the hollow of your hand to roll the meat mixture around.

7.

For the dip sauce, simply mix all the ingredients together until smooth. Season with salt and pepper.

Calories	Protein	Carbs	sugar	Total Fat	Sat Fat	Fiber
54	6g	3g	0.8g	2g	0.5g	1g

Per lollipop.

PEEK-A-BOO HOT DOG

Total time: 35 min.
Prep: 10 min.
Cook: 25 min.
Yield: 10 slices.

Ingredients:

1 cup whole-grain rice flour.
1 cup rye flour.
2 cups almond milk (unsweetened).
2 large eggs.
1 tablespoon baking-powder.
½ teaspoon salt.

For the hot dogs:

10 reduced fat turkey sausages.
1 medium-yellow onion, sliced.
1 large tomato, chopped.
½ cup sweet corn.
¼ cup green peas.
2 tablespoons tomato paste.
½ cup water.
2 tablespoons low-fat Parmesan cheese.
2 tablespoons parsley, chopped (optional).
Salt and pepper to taste.

1. Preheat oven to 390 °F (198 °C). Lightly grease a 10″x10″ (25 x 25 cm) baking-pan with cooking-spray.

2.

Poke small holes in each sausage with a fork to let the air out as they cook.

4.

In a blender, place the milk, eggs, flours, salt and baking-powder and blend for 1 minute. Turn off blender and with a plastic spatula push the excess flour on the edges of the blender into the mix. Turn blender on again and blend for 2 more minutes until smooth.

3.

Cook sausages in boiling water for 3 minutes, this process will reduce the sodium content and fat.

5.

In a frying pan with cooking-spray, over medium-high heat, stir-fry sliced onion and chopped tomato, let it cook for 2 minutes and turn off heat. Add the sweet corn, green peas, tomato paste, water and season with salt and pepper to taste, mix and set aside.

6.

Lay half of the batter on the prepared baking pan spreading evenly across the bottom. Place sausages as shown in the photo.

7.

Cover sausages with tomato mixture.

8.

Finish up blanketing with the remaining batter spreading well and covering all the sausages. Top with grated Parmesan and sprinkles of chopped parsley. Bake for 25-30 minutes or until you see significant color. To make sure that it is fully baked, insert a toothpick in the center of the cake. If it comes out clean it is ready. Let it cool down and serve.

Calories	Protein	Carbs	sugar	Total Fat	Sat Fat	Fiber
206	8g	25g	2g	8g	2g	3g

CANOE PIZZA

Total time: 22 min.
Prep: 7 min.
Cook: 15 min.
Yield: 4 portions.

Ingredients:

2 summer squash zucchinis.
2 tablespoons tomato sauce.
24 slices, low-fat turkey pepperoni.
½ cup low-fat Mexican four cheese, grated.
2 teaspoons dry oregano.
12 cherry tomatoes, sliced.
½ small red onion, sliced.

1. Preheat oven 400 °F (204 °C).

2.

Take zucchinis, trim stems and slice lengthwise.

3.

Flatten bottom by removing a thin slice so it will sit level on baking-tray.

6.

Bake for 15 minutes on an ungreased baking-sheet.

4.

Cut cherry tomatoes in 4 pieces and slice onion. Set aside.

5.

Gently spread tomato sauce on each zucchini then add cheese, sliced onion, pepperoni, sliced cherry tomatoes and finish with sprinkles of dry oregano.

Calories	Protein	Carbs	sugar	Total Fat	Sat Fat	Fiber
110	7g	9g	5g	5g	2g	3g

MAC & CHEESE
WITH PETIT MEATBALLS

Total time: 35 min.
Prep: 20 min.
Cook: 15 min.
Yield: 5 portions.

Ingredients:

2 cups whole-wheat elbow macaroni.
⅓ cup almond meal/flour (for topping).

For the petite meatballs:

1 lb. (453 g) 93% lean ground beef.
1 medium yellow onion, chopped.
¼ cup parsley, chopped.
½ cup green onion, chopped.
½ teaspoon reduced sodium seasoned salt.
1 tablespoon yellow mustard.
1 tablespoon Worcestershire sauce.
2 garlic cloves, minced.

For the cheese sauce:

1 cup fat-free cream cheese
1 container fat-free Greek yogurt
½ cup unsweetened almond milk
½ teaspoon paprika
1 teaspoon onion powder
½ cup grated low-fat cheddar cheese
1 teaspoon cornstarch
½ teaspoon salt
1 pinch nutmeg (optional)

1. Preheat oven to 400 °F (204 °C). Bring a large pot with hot water and place pasta and cook according to the pasta package directions. While pasta is cooking, start chopping onion, parsley, green onions and mince garlic.

2.

In a large bowl, place ground beef, chopped onion, minced garlic, chopped parsley, chopped green onion, mustard, Worcestershire sauce and seasoned salt. Mix well until well-combined.

4.

To make the cheese sauce: In a large microwave-safe bowl, add cream cheese to the milk and microwave for 1 minute. Remove from microwave and add the Greek yogurt, paprika, onion powder, corn-starch, cheddar cheese, salt and nutmeg. Mix well until creamy.

3.

Grease your hands with cooking spray and make small, bite-size meatballs by using the palm of your hand to roll the meat mixture around. Place on a baking-pan and bake for 4 minutes.

5.

In a separate large bowl, place cooked macaroni and pour the cheese sauce, mixing well.

6.

Heat a frying pan over medium-high heat (no grease needed), place almond flour, mixing constantly, and cook for 1 minute until golden-brown as shown in the photo.

7.

In an oven-safe large skillet or any baking dish, place macaroni and cheese and half of the meatballs.

8.

Finish with another layer of macaroni and cheese and meatballs, and finish up with toasted almond flour. Bake for 5 minutes. Finish up with chopped green onions on top.

Calories	Protein	Carbs	sugar	Total Fat	Sat Fat	Fiber
444	39g	43g	6g	13g	4g	6g

CARROT CUPCAKES
WITH CHOCOLATE CREAM CHEESE FROSTING

Total time: 30 min.
Prep: 10 min.
Cook: 20 min.
Yield: 12 cupcakes.

Ingredients:

3 large carrots, peeled and grated.
4 eggs.
2 cups gluten-free all-purpose flour.
2 teaspoons organic stevia.
½ cup unsweetened vanilla almond milk.
½ teaspoon turmeric.
2 teaspoons baking-powder.
1 cup no-sugar-added apple sauce.
4 tablespoon dark chocolate 85% cocoa, chopped.

Chocolate Frosting:

5.29 oz. (150 g) 85% dark chocolate.
5.29 oz. (150 g) cream cheese (room temperature).
1 teaspoon organic stevia.

Tips: You may substitute stevia with agave use (¼ cup) the same amount for brown sugar or honey (calories may increase). You may also use cupcakes paper cups for this recipe.

1. Preheat oven to 350 °F (175 °C) and grease a muffin pan with cooking-spray.

2.

Wash and Slice carrots very thinly, place into a microwave safe plate separately as shown.

3.

microwave for 1-2 minutes or until you see carrots curling and shaping into "flowers". Set aside.

4.

Grate carrots. (If using organic carrots, there is no need to peel) Chop 50g dark chocolate into small bits. Set aside.

5.

In a large bowl, whisk together eggs, flour, stevia/agave, almond milk, turmeric, applesauce, chocolate bits, grated carrots and finally baking powder. Mix well until all combined.

6.

Pour the batter into muffin cavities and bake for 15-20 minutes.

7.

While cupcakes are baking, start making the ganache. In a medium microwave-safe bowl, place dark chocolate and microwave for 1 minute, then add cream cheese into melted chocolate, stevia and mix well. Set aside. Decorate cupcakes with chocolate frosting and carrot flowers.

Calories	Protein	Carbs	sugar	Total Fat	Sat Fat	Fiber
216	7g	26g	8g	8g	4g	1g

GOBBLE GOBBLE BURGER

Total time: 20 min.
Prep: 10 min.
Cook: 10 min.
Yield: 12 mini burgers.

Ingredients:

1 lb. (453g) lean 93% ground turkey.
½ green zucchini, grated.
½ yellow zucchini, grated.
½ cup broccoli, chopped.
½ orange bell pepper, chopped.
1 tablespoon Worcestershire sauce.
1 tablespoon yellow mustard.
3 slices cheddar cheese.
2 tomatoes, sliced.
½ teaspoon seasoned sauce.
1 cup spring salad mix.
12 whole grain sliders mini buns.
12 bamboo knot picks (Optional)

Tip: Serve this burger with carrot mayo or avocado mayo on the dips and sauces section.

1.

Chop bell pepper and broccoli in small pieces, then shred zucchinis.

3.

Lay down plastic wrap or aluminum foil, lightly grease with cooking spray then shape mixture into 12 mini balls, place over pre-greased side then press down using your fingers to form mini burgers.

2.

In a large bowl mix: ground turkey, vegetables, mustard, Worcestershire sauce, and seasoned salt. Mix well until well combined.

4.

Lightly grease a frying pan with cooking spray, cook mini burgers for 2 minutes each side over medium heat.

5.

Cut cheddar cheese in 4 small squares and place over each mini burgers.

6.

Cover the frying pan to melt the cheese and finish the coking. Let it cover for 2 more minutes.

7.

Build the mini burgers by adding the greens first (this will prevent your buns from becoming soggy) then the tomatoes, and finally the turkey burgers.

Calories	Protein	Carbs	sugar	Total Fat	Sat Fat	Fiber
171	12g	15g	2g	7g	2g	3g

APPLE CHOCOLATE POPSICLE

Total time: 15 min.
Prep: 5 min.
Cook: 10 min.
Yield: 6 popsicles.

Ingredients:

2 large pink lady apples.
3.5 oz. (100 g) dark chocolate - 70% cocoa.
2 tablespoons, all natural peanut butter.
1 tablespoon, pecan sprinkles.
1 tablespoon, pumpkin kernels.
1 tablespoon, sunflower kernels.
2 tablespoons, natural raisins.
2 tablespoons, shredded coconut unsweetened.

1.

Cover a flat plate with aluminum foil or plastic wrap and lightly spray with cooking spray.

3.

Cut apples lengthwise in slices as seem in the photo.

2.

In a medium microwave safe bowl add chocolate pieces and peanut butter, microwave for 1 minute. Stir well until all chocolate pieces are completely melted.

4.

Insert the tip of a knife into the bottom of the slice to make space for the Popsicle stick (see photo).

5.

Insert Popsicle stick until you feel that it is firm and will hold. Pat dry slices before coating with the melted chocolate.

6.

Pour melted chocolate over a plate and start covering apples, as seen in the photo.

7.

Finish decorating with seeds, coconut flakes and raisins. Place popsicles in the freezer for 5 minutes before serving.

Calories	Protein	Carbs	sugar	Total Fat	Sat Fat	Fiber
187	3g	19g	13g	11g	5g	4g

DESSERTS

PEANUT & CHOCOLATE DONUTS

Total time: 35 min.
Prep: 10 min.
Cook: 25 min.
Yield: 12 donuts.

Ingredients:

1 cup brown-rice flour.
½ cup almond flour.
2 tablespoons flax seed.
½ cup peanut-butter powder.
½ cup vanilla whey protein (optional).
1 and ½ teaspoons organic stevia.
2 teaspoons baking-powder.
2 cups unsweetened almond milk.
2 large eggs.
2 teaspoons pure vanilla extract.

For the topping:

⅓ cup unsalted peanuts, chopped.
3.5 oz. (100g) dark chocolate 70% cocoa.

Tips: If you use dark chocolate for topping, add a pinch of organic stevia when it is melted to add some sweetness to it. You may also use chocolate or any other whey protein flavor for the batter.

1. Preheat oven to 350 °F (176 °C). Lightly grease a 12 cavity donut pan.

2.

In a large bowl, mix brown-rice flour, almond flour, flax seed, peanut powder, whey protein, stevia, and baking-powder. Set aside.

4.

Combine flour mix with almond milk and eggs, mix very well and make sure that the mixture has no lumps.

3.

In a small bowl, lightly beat eggs and add vanilla extract.

5.

Pour the batter into a piping bag (or re-sealable bag, cutting a corner large enough to pour the batter. Fill ¾ of each cavity with the batter.

6.

Bake donuts for 20 minutes.

7.

Chop chocolate in small pieces and melt in the microwave for 1 minute. Spread melted chocolate over each donut and sprinkle chopped peanuts on top.

Calories	Protein	Carbs	sugar	Total Fat	Sat Fat	Fiber
224	10g	19g	3g	12g	2g	3g

RASPBERRY CAKE
WITH VANILLA YOGURT FROSTING

Total time: 40 min.
Prep: 10 min.
Cook: 30 min.
Yield: 10 Slices.

Ingredients:

2 cups almond flour.
½ cup coconut flour.
4 large eggs.
½ tablespoon organic stevia.
2 tablespoons organic agave.
1 and ½ teaspoons vanilla extract.
1 and ½ cups unsweetened almond milk.
2 teaspoons baking-powder.
1 cup fresh raspberries.

For the topping:

1 (5oz) container fat-free vanilla yogurt.
2 tablespoons roasted pistachios.
½ cup Fresh raspberries.
Mint leaves.

Tips: Raspberries are not very sweet so, if you want a sweeter cake, substitute for chopped strawberries.

1. Preheat oven to 390 °F (198 °C). Grease a 9" x 4.5" bread-loaf pan with cooking-spray.

2.
In a large bowl, mix the dry ingredients using a metal whisk.

3.
Whisk milk, eggs, agave and vanilla, then add the dry ingredients from step 2.

6.
Add raspberries on top of first layer of batter. Complete by covering and filling the pan with the remaining half of the batter.

4.
Using a spatula, fold and mix all the ingredients until you achieve a lump-free batter.

5.
Pour half of the batter into a prepared loaf-pan and spread well.

7.
Bake for 30 minutes. Let the cake cool down and start decorating by first spreading the yogurt on top and then garnishing with raspberries, pistachios and mint leaves.

Calories	Protein	Carbs	sugar	Total Fat	Sat Fat	Fiber
238	10g	18g	7g	14g	2g	7g

PIÑA COLADA CREAM

Total time: 25 min.
Prep: 10 min.
Cook: 15 min.
Yield: 4 servings.

Ingredients:

2 cups unsweetened almond milk.
1 tablespoon corn-starch.
1 cup unsweetened coconut flakes.
½ cup 100% natural coconut water.
½ teaspoon organic stevia.
1 tablespoon unflavored gelatin.

For pineapple topping:

2 cups ripe fresh pineapple, chopped.
¼ cup 100% natural coconut water.
Mint leaves.
Cocktail umbrellas.

1. In a small, microwave-safe container, place a tablespoon of water and heat for 10 seconds. Take out and add the gelatin mix until dissolved.

2.
Dissolve corn-starch in 3 tablespoons almond milk.

4.
Add the coconut flakes and the liquid gelatin. Mix well.

3.
In a medium saucepan over medium-high heat, combine almond milk / corn starch mix, coconut water and stevia. Slowly bring to a boil and heat for about 5 minutes until it starts to thicken.

5.
Let the cream cool down to room temperature then pour into four glasses and let it set in the fridge until firm.

6.
Chop pineapple into small cubes.

7.
In a medium saucepan, add the two cups chopped pineapple, ¼ cup coconut water and 3-4 mint leaves and let it cook for 3 minutes. Once done, let it cool.

8.
Place chopped pineapples carefully over the coconut cream, garnish with a mint leaf and cocktail umbrella.

Calories	Protein	Carbs	sugar	Total Fat	Sat Fat	Fiber
224	3g	21g	11g	14g	9g	5g

VANILLA PEAR
WITH CHOCOCONUT FALL

Total time: 15 min.
Prep: 10 min.
Cook: 50 min.
Yield: 2 servings.

Ingredients:

2 medium, firm ripe pears.
1 tablespoon vanilla extract.
3 tablespoons water.
2 ounces (57g) dark chocolate 85% cocoa.
¼ cup light coconut milk.
½ teaspoon organic stevia.
2 tablespoons chopped pecans or peanuts.

1. Remove pear bottoms making them sit straight, then remove pear seeds by making a little hole inside with the tip of knife as shown in the photo.

3. To shape the pears: Using a small knife, mark 3 little dots: a) one inch from the bottom, b) two inches from the bottom in the middle and c) 3 inches from the bottom on top. Now, using the dots as guides carefully slice pears in diagonal on the left and right meting each dot.

2. In a microwave-safe plate, place vanilla extract and water and sit pears in the liquid. Cook in the microwave for 2 minutes and let it cool. This process will cook pears and allow vanilla extract to infuse inside pears.

4. You should end up with each pear cut into 3 "V" shaped sections as shown in the photo.

5. Return cut pears to their original shape by sliding each section back as shown in the photo.

6.

In a small microwave-safe bowl, place dark chocolate broken into pieces (to facilitate melting) and microwave for 1 minute. Add coconut milk, stevia and mix well.

7.

Cover pears with melted chococonut and sprinkle chopped nuts on top.

Calories	Protein	Carbs	sugar	Total Fat	Sat Fat	Fiber
370	4g	39g	23g	22g	11g	10g

CLEMENTINE CAKE

Total time: 35 min.
Prep: 10 min.
Cook: 25 min.
Yield: 10 slices.

Ingredients:

½ cup clementine juice (about 4 clementines).

5 seedless clementines.

4 eggs.

3 and ½ cups almond flour.

3 and ½ teaspoons organic stevia.

2 teaspoons baking-powder.

½ cup unsweetened almond milk.

2 teaspoons vanilla extract.

1 tablespoon no-sugar-added orange marmalade/preserves.

2 tablespoons Unsweetened coconut flakes for topping (optional).

1. Preheat oven to 380 °F (193 °C) and lightly grease a 9″ (22cm) baking-pan with cooking-spray.

2.

Peel 2 clementines and squeeze the juice of 4.

3.

In a blender, blend peeled clementines into a paste and set aside.

6.

Dilute marmalade with 2 tablespoons of water.

4.

Whisk together blended clementine paste, almond flour, eggs, almond milk, vanilla extract, stevia and baking-powder. Mix well until very smooth.

5.

Pour the batter evenly into a prepared baking-pan and bake for 25 minutes.

7.

Garnish the baked cake with wedges of clementines and brush the diluted marmalade on top of each one as shown in the photo. This will give a shiny look and protect the fruit from drying out. Sprinkle coconut flakes on top.

Calories	Protein	Carbs	sugar	Total Fat	Sat Fat	Fiber
298	11g	19g	9g	20g	2g	5g

STRAWBERRY MOUSSE

Total time: 25 min.
Prep: 10 min.
Cook: 15 min.
Yield: 4 servings.

Ingredients:

½ lb. (226 g) fresh strawberries.
2 (5oz) containers plain fat-free yogurt.
½ cup light coconut milk.
¼ cup sliced almonds.
½ cup no-sugar-added strawberry preserves.
½ teaspoon stevia.
1 tablespoon water.
1 teaspoon unflavored gelatin.

Tip: You may change the fruit flavor by substituting with any other berry and no-sugar-added fruit preserve of your preference.(calories may change).

1. Wash strawberries, spread out onto a clean dishtowel and gently pat dry.

2.

Mix one tablespoon of water into the strawberry preserve and microwave for 15 seconds. Set aside.

3.

Remove the bottom of four strawberries and chop into small pieces, add to the preserve and mix well.

4.

In a small microwave-safe container, place 1 tablespoon water and heat for 10 seconds. Take out and add the gelatin mix until dissolved.

5.

To decorate the glasses slice strawberries as shown in the photo.

5.

In a bowl, mix yogurt, coconut milk, strawberry preserve, stevia, and gelatin. Stir gently and mix well.

6.

Start building the mousse by adding sliced almonds on the bottom, strawberries on the sides and the mousse in the middle. Finish with slices of almond and a whole strawberry on top. Place in the fridge to set for 20-30 minutes before serving.

Calories	Protein	Carbs	sugar	Total Fat	Sat Fat	Fiber
161	10g	19g	6g	5g	1g	2g

CHOCOPEANUT ICE CREAM

Total time: 10 min.
Prep: 7 min.
Cook: 3 min.
Yield: 5 Ice cream scoops.

Ingredients:

2 large ripe bananas.
½ cup low fat all natural peanut butter.
¾ cup unsweetened vanilla almond milk.
½ cup chocolate whey protein (low-carb/low-sugar).
1 tablespoon 85% cocoa chocolate, chopped.
½ teaspoon organic stevia.
2 tablespoons chopped peanuts (optional).

For the chocolate sauce:

4 tablespoons chocolate whey protein.
4 tablespoons water.
2 teaspoons unsweetened cocoa powder (optional).

1.

In a blender or food processor, place bananas, almond milk, peanut butter, whey protein and organic stevia. Blend for 2 minutes.

3.

In a small bowl, mix ice cream blended with chopped dark chocolate until well-combined.

2.

Finely chop dark chocolate. Set aside.

4.

Place ice cream mix in a covered plastic container and place in freezer. Ice Cream should set in 1 hour or so. (If you have a metal container with lid ice cream will set quicker.)

5.

For the chocolate sauce: mix protein-powder and unsweetened cocoa powder with 3 tablespoons of water, check if the consistency is creamy and if needed add 1 more tablespoon of water. Set aside in the refrigerator.

6.

Serve ice cream with chocolate sauce and chopped peanuts on top.

TIP: Use frozen bananas for this recipe if you want ice cream to set quicker.

Calories	Protein	Carbs	sugar	Total Fat	Sat Fat	Fiber
250	20g	25g	9g	14g	3g	4g

Per scoop.

APPLE CAKE
WITH COCONUT ORANGE SAUCE

Total time: 35 min.
Prep: 15 min.
Cook: 20 min.
Yield: 6 slices.

Ingredients:

3 eggs.
3 medium red apples.
1 teaspoon organic stevia.
1 cup almond flour.
½ cup all-purpose gluten-free flour.
2 tablespoons almond butter.
½ teaspoon ground cinnamon (Optional).
2 teaspoons baking-powder.

For the sauce:

½ teaspoon organic stevia.
1 cup no-sugar-added applesauce.
½ cup light coconut milk.
1 teaspoon cornstarch.
½ cup freshly squeezed orange juice.
2 cinnamon sticks for garnishing (optional).

1. Preheat oven to 390 °F (198 °C) and lightly grease a 10″ x 8″ (25cm x 20cm) baking-pan with cooking-spray.

2.

Peel 1 apple, remove the seeds and cut in small cubes. Set everything aside including the peel. Chop the other apple in large pieces.

3.

In a blender, add eggs, chopped apple, apple peels, flours, almond butter, cinnamon, and baking-powder. Blend for 3 minutes until smooth.

4.

In a medium bowl, mix the cake batter gently with the chopped apple.

5.

Spread the batter evenly on the prepared baking-pan and bake for 17 minutes.

6.

For the sauce: in a small sauce pan, add applesauce, orange juice, coconut milk, corn starch, stevia and mix well until cornstarch is fully dissolved.

7.

Bring to a boil over medium heat until it starts to thicken, turn off the heat and let it cool down.

8.

Spread the sauce over the baked cake and decorate with sliced apple to your liking.

Calories	Protein	Carbs	sugar	Total Fat	Sat Fat	Fiber
306	10g	35g	16g	13g	3g	7g

CHERRY CAKE

Total time: 30 min.
Prep: 10 min.
Cook: 20 min.
Yield: 8 slices.

Ingredients:

½ cup brown rice flour.
½ cup almond flour.
2 large eggs.
½ cup light coconut milk.
2 teaspoons baking powder.
1 tablespoon organic stevia.
½ cup unsweetened coconut flakes.

For the topping:

1 cup low-fat/low sugar vanilla yogurt.
1 ounce (28 g) dark chocolate, 85% cocoa.
1 teaspoon organic stevia.
1 cup fresh cherries.

1. Preheat oven to 390 °F (198 °C) and lightly grease a 8x1 (20 cm) inch baking pan with cooking-spray.

2.

In a blender, place coconut milk, eggs, flours, organic stevia, coconut flakes, and baking powder. Blend for 2 minutes.

3.

Pour the blended mixture into prepared baking pan.

4.

Spread the batter evenly with a spoon and bake for 20 minutes.

5.

To check if the cake is fully cooked insert a toothpick in the center of the cake, if it comes out clean it's ready, if not bake for an additional 5 minutes.

6.

Cut cherries in half, remove stems and pits and set cherry halves aside in the refrigerator.

7.

In a microwave-safe container, melt dark chocolate for 1 minutes then mix with 1 teaspoon organic stevia. Top cake with yogurt, spreading with spoon, and top with cherries and drizzled melted chocolate on top.

Calories	Protein	Carbs	sugar	Total Fat	Sat Fat	Fiber
199	6g	19g	2g	11g	5g	3g

AVOCADO ORANGE PARFAIT

Total time: 12 min.
Prep: 7 min.
Cook: 5 min.
Yield: 2 portions.

Ingredients:

1 cup wheat flakes cereal.
1 large avocado.
½ cup freshly squeezed orange juice.
½ cup unsweetened almond milk.
1 tablespoon roasted sunflower kernels.
½ teaspoon organic stevia.

1. Using the bottom of a glass, crush cereal into small pieces.

2. Peel the orange, saving the skin for garnishing.

3. In a blender place avocado pulp, orange juice, almond milk, and stevia. Blend for 2 minutes until smooth.

4. To build parfaits: Layer first cereal then avocado parfait, repeating the process until you fill ¾ of the glass. Finish up with ½ teaspoon of sunflower kernels and a twisted orange skin as shown in the photo. Serve cold.

Calories	Protein	Carbs	sugar	Total Fat	Sat Fat	Fiber
279	6g	31g	9g	16g	1g	9g

197

METRIC CONVERSION

VOLUME
MEASUREMENTS (DRY)

⅛ teaspoon = 0.5ml.

¼ teaspoon = 1 ml.

½ teaspoon = 2 ml.

¾ teaspoon = 4 ml.

1 tablespoon = 15 ml.

2 tablespoon = 30 ml.

¼ cup = 60 ml.

⅓ cup = 75 ml.

½ cup = 125 ml.

⅔ cup = 150 ml.

¾ cup = 175 ml.

1 cup = 250 ml.

2 cups = 500ml.

3 cups = 750 ml.

4 cups = 1 liter.

WEIGHTS (MASS)

½ ounce = 15 g.

1 ounce = 29 g.

3 ounces = 85 g.

4 ounces = 113 g.

8 ounces = 226 g.

10 ounces = 284 g.

12 ounces = 340 g.

16 ounces = 1 pound, 453 g.

DIMENSIONS

¼ inch = 6 mm.

½ inch = 1.5 cm.

¾ inch = 2 cm.

1 inch = 2.5 cm.

OVEN TEMPERATURES

250 °F = 120 °C.

275 °F = 140 °C.

300 °F = 150 °C.

325 °F = 160 °C.

350 °F = 180 °C.

375 °F = 190 °C.

400 °F = 200 °C.

425 °F = 220 °C.

450 °F = 230 °C.

BAKING PAN SIZES

SQUARE

8 x 8 x 1.5 inch = (20 x 20 x 4 cm) 6 cups (1.5 L)

8 x 8 x 2 inch = (20 x 20 x 5 cm) 8 cups (2 L)

9 x 9 x 1 1/2 inches = (23 x 23 x 4 cm) 8 cups (2 L)

9 x 9 x 2 inch = (23 x 23 x 5)10 cups (2.5 L)

10 x 10 x 2 inches = (25 x 25 x 5 cm)12 cups (3 L)

ROUND

6 x 2 inch (15 x 5) = 4 cups (1 L)

8 x 1.5 inch (20 x 4 cm) = 5 cups (1.2 L / 2 pints)

8 x 2 inch = (20 x 5 cm) 6 cups (1.5 L)

9 x 1.5 inch = (23 x 4 cm) 6 cups (1.5 L)

9 x 2 inch = (23 x 5 cm) 8 cups (2 L)

10 x 2 inch = (25 x 5 cm) 11 cups (2.6 L)

THANKS, OBRIGADO

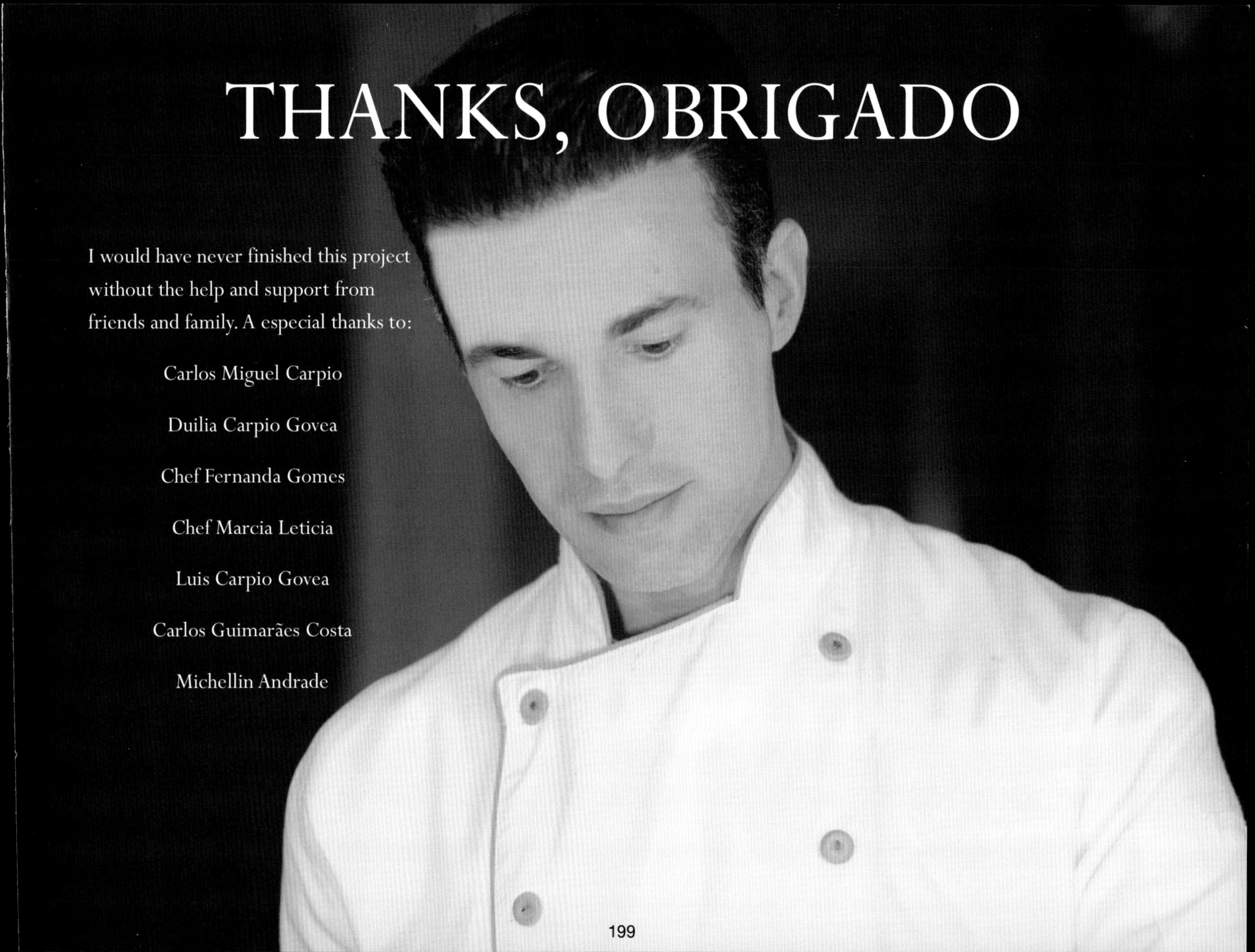

I would have never finished this project
without the help and support from
friends and family. A especial thanks to:

Carlos Miguel Carpio

Duilia Carpio Govea

Chef Fernanda Gomes

Chef Marcia Leticia

Luis Carpio Govea

Carlos Guimarães Costa

Michellin Andrade

SUPERFOODS AND THEIR BENEFITS

A

Achiote paste (Annatto): Antioxidant, high in fiber, also helps lower cholesterol and manages diabetes.

Agave: Low-glycemic sweetener.

Allspice: Anti-inflammatory helps to improve blood circulation, Immune system booster, and aids in digestion.

Almond flour: High in fiber, good source of protein, and gluten free.

Almond milk: Low calorie, free of cholesterol, saturated fat, and lactose free, and good source of protein.

Almond: Source of Healthy fats, fiber, protein, magnesium and vitamin E, Helps lower blood pressure, blood sugar levels and lower cholesterol level.

Apple cider vinegar: Kills bacteria, antibiotic properties, helps prevent intestinal discomfort, aids in lowering blood sugar levels, helps lower cholesterol, and good source of potassium.

Applesauce, all natural: Good source of natural fiber, and vitamin C.

Asparagus: Good source of fiber, vitamins A, C, E and K, antioxidant, and a natural diuretic.

Avocado: High in fiber, lowers cholesterol and triglyceride levels, high in potassium, reduce LDL (bad) cholesterol and increase HDL (good) cholesterol

B

Balsamic vinegar: Antioxidant, Improves body immunity, good source of calcium, iron, magnesium and potassium.

Banana: Antioxidant, Good source of potassium, Fiber, vitamin B6, vitamin C, and supports our overall digestive system.

Basil: Anti-inflammatory, antioxidant, liver protector.

Beet: Lowers blood pressure, anti-inflammatory, anti-cancer properties, rich in vitamin C, Stamina booster and detoxification support.

Bell pepper: Low caloric, high in vitamin C, good source of vitamin E and B6.

Black beans: High in protein, fiber, potassium, vitamin B6, folate, copper, iron, and high in antioxidants.

Black olives: Rich in fat acids and antioxidants, promotes digestive health, and important source of vitamin E. (Not recommended for a low sodium diet.)

Blueberry: Rich in fiber, vitamin C, Vitamin K and manganese.

Broccoli: Strengthens bones, protects your heart, and controls blood pressure.

Brown rice: Gluten free, full of fiber, and rich in selenium and manganese.

Brussels sprouts: Anti-oxidant, anti-cancer, anti-inflammatory, promotes health bones and high in vitamin C.

Bulgur wheat: Good source of protein, vitamin B, magnesium, iron, and niacin. High in fiber, Iron, low GI, aids weight loss, good source of protein, manganese and folate.

Black pepper. Improves kidney function, improves liver function, source of manganese, iron, vitamin K, fiber and copper.

C

Cabbage: Detoxifies stomach and colon, stimulates immune system, blood cleanser, and aids weight loss.

Capers: Antioxidant, contain mineral like iron, calcium and copper. (Not recommended for a low sodium diet.)

Carrot: Protect against prostate cancer, improves immune system, improves eyesight, protect liver, reduces cholesterol, rich in beta-carotene and vitamin A.

Catfish: High in protein, Contains healthy fatty acids such as Omega-3 and Omega-6.

Cauliflower: Protects against prostate cancer, combats breast cancer, and strengthens bones, good source of vitamin C, K, B6, and minerals such as potassium and manganese.

Cayenne pepper: Aids with digestion, improves circulation, lower blood pressure, fight cold and flu, and aids with weight loss.

Celery: Anti-Cancer, calms nerves, lower blood pressure, rids kidney of gall stones, rich in vitamin K, A, C and B6.

Cheese: Strength immune system, strengthens bones, reduces risk of osteoporosis in post-menopausal woman.

Cherry tomatoes: Lowers cholesterol, promotes prostate health, high in vitamin C and A, high in calcium and potassium.

Cherry: Promotes liver health, helps fight cancer, aids weight loss, anti-aging, great source of vitamin A.

Chicken breast: Rich in lean, high quality protein, aids in growth and development of muscles, lowers risk of cholesterol and heart disorders.

Chickpeas: High in fiber, Iron, low glycemic index, aids weight loss, good source of protein, manganese and folate.

Chipotle: Aids in weight loss, helps improve the immune system, rich in anti-inflammatory properties.

Chives: helps detoxify the body, boosts immune system, rich in manganese, vitamin K, C, A, and folate.

Cilantro: Toxic metal cleansing, anti-inflammatory, aids in weight loss, lowers blood pressure, regulates blood sugar, aids digestion, promotes health liver function, anti-stress.

Cinnamon: Blood sugar control, food preservative, aid weight loss, lower LDL "bad" cholesterol and triglycerides.

Clementine (Tangerine & Mandarin): Low caloric, rich in fiber, potassium, calcium and vitamin C.

Cacao powder, Unsweetened: Rich in minerals such as: iron, manganese and zinc, antioxidant, increase energy and endurance, aids in weight loss, promotes healthy skin

Coconut flakes, unsweetened: Healthy fats, increases energy, improves cholesterol levels and reduces risks of heart disease, boosts brain function.

Coconut flour: Natural low in digestible carbohydrate, Gluten-free, high in fiber, protein and good fats.

Coconut milk: Boosts immune system, rich in antioxidants, aids weight control, calcium, vitamin B3, magnesium and phosphorus.

Coconut water: Balances your blood sugar, helps dissolve kidney stones, increase heart health, rich in magnesium.

Collard greens: Support the digestive system, beneficial for diabetics, provides healthy skin and hair, source of fiber, calcium, manganese, vitamin B-6, C, A and K.

Corn meal: Gluten-free, source of iron, phosphorus, and good source of fiber.

Corn: Controls diabetes and hypertension, prevents anemia, full of fiber, vitamin C and E.

Cottage cheese: Rich in protein, phosphorus, selenium, aids digestion, boosts immune system, helps to strengthen bones.

Couscous: Rich in antibacterial and antiviral properties, aids in weight management, vitamin B6, manganese, phosphorus, copper and magnesium.

Crabmeat: low in caloric and fat, rich in protein, provides selenium, aids thyroid function and helps build strong bones.

Cucumber: Reduces cholesterol, aids in weight loss, controls blood pressure and diabetes, contain vitamin B5, K and C.

Cumin: antioxidant, cancer fighter, lower blood pressure, helps remove toxins from body, prevent diabetes, vitamin B6, E and A, magnesium, iron, calcium and copper.

E

Egg whites: Low caloric, high quality complete protein, contain all essential amino acids, zero cholesterol, and easy to digest.

Egg (whole): Contains 9 essential amino acids, high quality protein, vitamin D, A, B2, B6, B12 and folic acid and minerals such as iron, calcium, potassium and phosphorus.

Eggplant: Fights cancer, promotes digestive health, helps improve skin quality, promotes weight loss, rich in fiber, vitamin C, potassium, magnesium, calcium and phosphorus.

Extra virgin Olive oil (uncooked): anti-inflammatory properties, antioxidant, helps prevent cancer, lowers "bad" cholesterol, lowers blood pressure.

F

Flax seed: Omega-3 essential fat acids, potent anti-inflammatory, prevent colon cancer, breast cancer, and colon cleanser, reduce heart-attack risk, contains vitamin B, improves blood sugar and its high in fiber.

G

Garbanzo beans: High in fiber, Iron, low GI, aids weight loss, good source of protein, manganese and folate.

Garlic: Strengthens immune system, has vitamin C and B6, regulates blood sugar and blood pressure, kills urinary tract infections, kills cold sores, removes heavy metals from the body, increases insulin production, has selenium, manganese, iron and calcium.

Gelatin (unflavored): Helps aid digestion, improves skin collagen, can help joint recovery and can help tighten loose skin.

Ginger: Controls diabetes, treats migraine, suppresses cough, treats and prevents multiple forms of cancer, cures menstrual pain/cramps and morning sickness, boost immune system.

Greek yogurt: Great source of protein, Probiotics, easy to digest, aids weight loss and digestion.

Green apple: Anti-oxidants, potassium, zinc, copper, vitamin B6, C, reduces LDL (bad) cholesterol, lower risk of diabetes type 2.

Green olives: Contain healthy monounsaturated fat, vitamin E, (not recommended for a low sodium diet)

Green onion: Control blood pressure, immune system booster, rich in vitamin C, helps regulates blood sugar and lower "bad" cholesterol.

Green peas: Aids liver function, high in fiber, good source of protein, vitamin C, A, and magnesium.

Green tomatillo: Helps to improve digestive health, regulates blood sugar levels, reduce bad cholesterol, boosts immune system and rich in vitamins C and K.

H

Heart of palm: Good source of dietary fiber, and protein (A bit high in sodium not recommended for a low sodium diet)

Hot sauce: Aids with weight loss, increase energy levels and speed metabolism, regulates blood sugar and helps relieve congestion.

J

Jalapeño: Fights migraine and sinus headaches, reduce risk of cancer, natural fat burner, and heal inflammations.

K

Kale: Aids with weight loss, high in protein, aids detoxification, fights cancer, improves bone health, low carb, rich in Iron, calcium, vitamin C, K and a great anti-inflammatory.

Kiwi: Low glycemic index (GI), aids with weight loss, rich in vitamins A, C, and K and minerals such as calcium, potassium and magnesium.

L

Leek: Rich in fiber, lowers blood pressure, lower cholesterol levels, anti-inflammatory and a natural diuretic.

Lemon: Boosts immune system, rich in vitamin C, relieves respiratory problems, aids in digestion, and helps remove toxins from the body.

Lime: Helps in digestion, aids in weight loss, more vitamin vitamin C than lemon, high in anti-oxidants, lowers blood pressure

Lobster meat: Rich source of copper, zinc, phosphorus and selenium, vitamin B12, and E.

M

Mango: regulates thyroid, aids digestion, source of vitamin E, vitamin A, and antioxidant.

Mint: Helps respiratory disorders and coughs, controls asthma, helps digestion, and weight loos.

Mustard: Helps to prevent cancer, reduces risk of cardiovascular diseases, helps managing diabetes and cholesterol levels.

N

Nutmeg: Helps to lower blood pressure, eliminate toxins from body, dissolve kidney stones and provides relief from insomnia, rich in folate and manganese.

O

Oatmeal: Controls blood sugar, blood pressure, helps lower bad cholesterol, rich in minerals and vitamins, good energy source.

Okra: Protects from stomach ulcers, great for weight loss, rich in amino acids, lowers bad cholesterol, prevents liver disease.

Orange: Helps maintain skin health and vision, supports respiratory health, and helps lower blood pressure, great source of vitamin C and fiber.

Oregano: Combats bacterial infections, powerful antiviral and anti bacterial.

P

Paprika: Rich in vitamin E, regulates blood pressure, antioxidant, improves circulation, lowers the risk of cancer.

Parsley: Anti-inflammatory, antibacterial, anti-oxidant, prevent anemia, digestive aid, kidney health, and vitamins K, C and A.

Peach: Rich in fiber and antioxidants, improves kidney function, prevents against anemia, rich in vitamin A, C, K and B, also a good source of dietary fiber.

Peanut butter, all natural: High in fiber, vitamin E, protein, and helps lower "bad" cholesterol.

Peanuts (Unsalted): Protects from heart disease, good source of protein, Contain good fats, rich in vitamin E and fiber.

Pear: Lower blood pressure; helps prevent cancer, energy booster, high in fiber and vitamin C, and potassium.

Pecan: Aid with weight loss, cancer preventer, heart health, prostate health, high in antioxidants, and lower "bad" cholesterol

Pepper: Assists in breakdown of fat cells, aids weight loss, and facilitates digestion.

Pickles: Helps weight loss, low in calories, carbs and fat, good source of fiber (High in sodium not recommended for a low sodium diet)

Pineapple: Natural diuretic, lowers blood pressure, combats cancer, helps heal inflammation, anti-aging, good source of beta carotene, vitamins C and B9, and minerals such as copper, potassium and iron.

Poblano chili: high in fiber, rich in iron and vitamin A.

Poppy seed: improves heart health, prevents bone damage, boosts immunity, rich in minerals such as zinc, magnesium, copper, potassium and iron.

Pork loin (lean): Good source of high quality protein, source of essential minerals such as selenium and phosphorus.

Portobello mushroom: Low caloric, high in fiber, source of protein and low in carbohydrates, also minerals such as potassium and phosphorus.

Pumpkin kernel: lower cholesterol, high in omega-3, reduces level of LDL "bad" cholesterol, good for prostate health and high in zinc.

Pumpkin: improves bladder and prostate health, controls blood sugar, omega 3-fats, anti-inflammatory benefits, and high in fiber, vitamin A and potassium.

Q

Quinoa: high protein content, low glycemic index (GI), aids in weight-loss, high in fiber, and minerals such as manganese, folate, and phosphorus.

R

Radish: Treats urinary disorders, promotes digestion, improves bone health, rich in fiber, vitamin C, K, B, and calcium, cooper, zinc and iron.

Raisin, all natural: Reduces blood pressure, helps in digestion, and helps against anemia, source of iron, copper, and potassium.

Raspberry: Prevent bladder infection, high in fiber, high in antioxidants, source of vitamin C, B3, K and minerals such as copper, manganese and iron.

Red apple: Cancer prevention, Alzheimer's prevention, antioxidant benefits, good source of vitamin C, and fiber.

Red onion: Helps prevent cardiovascular disease, dissolve blood clots, help detoxify the body, reduce blood pressure, source of vitamin C and B6, improves immunity and digestive system.

Red potato: Boosts immune system, supports muscle function, lowers cholesterol, and provides energy, high in fiber, vitamin B, iron and potassium.

Red wine vinegar: Controls blood sugar, promotes weight loss, and lowers cholesterol.

Ricotta cheese: Good source of protein, calcium, selenium and vitamins A and B12.

Romaine lettuce: Low caloric, antioxidant, rich in vitamin C and fiber, high water content, helps lower blood pressure.

Russet potato: Source of vitamin B6 and C, Fiber, and minerals such as magnesium, iron zinc and phosphorus.

Rye flour: Lowers diabetes type 2 risks, full of fiber, high in protein and essential amino acids, less caloric than wheat flour.

S

Salmon: Good source of high quality protein, reduces risk of cardiovascular diseases, aids in healthy skin and hair, rich in vitamins B12, B6, and minerals such as selenium, phosphorus, and potassium.

Salt: Allows nutrient absorption, maintain the fluid balance in the body and proper stomach pH, balances hormones. (Excess of salt is not recommended for people with high blood pressure).

Sardines: Cancer prevention, omega-3 fatty acids, anti-inflammatory, helps promotes healthy cholesterol, high in vitamin B12, promotes bone health.

Sesame seeds: Lower cholesterol, High in protein, ant-inflammatory, assists digestion, and good source of vitamin B.

Shrimp: Low in fat, high quality protein, aids in improving memory performance, decrease risk of diabetes, excellent source of selenium and vitamin B12.

Soybeans: Excellent source of fiber, helps prevent osteoporosis, improves blood circulation and heart health, high in protein, vitamins K, and B6, and minerals such as manganese and phosphorus.

Spinach: High in fiber, antioxidants, low blood sugar, high in iron, and vitamins A, B and C.

Stevia: Aids in managing diabetes, aids in weight loss, helps to prevent cavities and gingivitis, zero calories, stevia plant is high in fiber, iron, vitamin A and C.

Strawberry: Helps regulates proper function of nervous system, boosts immune system, rich in vitamin C, reduces inflammation, and aids in weight loss.

Sunflower kernel: Improves bone health, antioxidant, and rich in vitamin E, copper, iron, and magnesium.

Sweet pepper: Anti-inflammatory, lowers bad cholesterol, filled with vitamin C, and beta-carotene.

Sweet potatoes: Anti-inflammatory, aids in weight loss, rich in vitamin C, E, B-6 and beta-carotene, good source of energy, high in fiber and protein.

T

Tilapia: Good source of high quality protein, easy to digest, aids in weight loss, high in vitamins B12 and Niacin, and minerals such as selenium, phosphorus and potassium.

Tomato: Support bone health, reduce heart disease, lowers cholesterol, boosts immune system, and good amount of vitamin C, A and B6.

Turkey bacon: Good source of protein, low in saturated fat, and provides vitamin B-12, aids in weight loss.

Turkey ham: Good source of protein, low in saturated fat, provides vitamin B-12, and aids in weight loss.

Turkey: Rich source of protein, low in fat, aids in weight loss, reduce LDL "bad" cholesterol, and rich in vitamin B-12.

Turmeric: Helps prevent cancer, treats depression, and lowers cholesterol, controls diabetes, prevent liver disease, reduces cholesterol, controls blood pressure, anti-inflammatory, and very strong antioxidant.

V

Vanilla extract: Immune system booster, antioxidant, aids in weight loss, relieves nausea, and antibacterial properties.

W

Whey protein powder: Great source of fast release protein and amino acids, helps control hunger, promotes fat loss, and helps build stronger bones and muscles.

Whole grain pasta: high in fiber, high in protein, helps lower cholesterol, aids in weight loss, and keeps you full longer.

Whole-grain rice flour: Gluten free, source of protein, rich in fiber, rich in selenium and manganese, promotes weight loss.

Y

Yam: Anti-inflammatory, aids in weight loss, rich in vitamin C, E, B-6 and beta-carotene, good source of energy, high in fiber and protein.

Yellow curry: Excellent source of iron and manganese, anti-inflammatory, source of vitamin B6, and copper and potassium.

Yellow onion: Anti-inflammatory, good source of biotin, manganese, vitamin B6, C, and dietary fiber.

Z

Zucchini: high in protein, fiber, vitamin C, low caloric, anti-oxidant, anti-inflammatory properties, and high in water content.

"I believe Super food is: the food that you eat and you feel well after words, feel light, full or energy, feel healthy and promotes well-being. Especially when is prepared by you for you."

Authors Note: it is important that you take into account the advice on the chapter " food labels 101"(pg. 15). In order to cook my recipes for this book I sourced the healthiest and leanest ingredients I could find in common supermarket chains, and I have specifically avoided recommending or mentioning any of these by brand because it will simply make it more difficult for you to start cooking. Nonetheless you can achieve the same, if not very similar results, by being intelligent and observant of the ingredients you are buying. Always look at the food labels and if you see that, food portions being equal, you can purchase something that has less fat, carbohydrates, sugar or salt or more protein. Always go for the healthier option and you can't go wrong.

VITAMINS

	FUNCTIONS	SOURCES
A	Health teeth, skin, bones, and eyes.	Eggs, milk, dark green leafy vegetables, squash, carrots,
B	Energy production, digest proteins, proper functioning of central nervous system.	Lean meats, eggs, dairy products, fish, soybeans, cabbage, whole grains.
C	Helps immune system, skin, teeth, hair.	Citrus fruits, bell peppers, broccoli, guava, tomatoes, papaya, kiwi.
D	Helps absorb calcium, health bones, teeth, immune system.	Dairy products, oysters, fish, sunlight.
E	Skin, vision, hair, protects red blood cells.	Corn, nuts, olives, green leafs vegetables, sunflower seeds, wheat germ.
K	Health bones, blood clotting.	Cauliflower, spinach, cabbage, soybeans, kale, broccoli.

Proteins- Are used to build and repair tissues, such as bones, muscles, cartilage, skin and blood. Amino acids are the basic building blocks of protein and are classified as essential for muscle building. Look always for lean sources of protein, such as poultry and fish and lean meats.

Carbohydrates- Gives your body energy and works as a fuel for the central nervous system and working muscles. Try to eat good sources of carbs avoiding simple carbs such as white flour.

Fats- Fat is a concentrated source of energy; fat also helps you absorb vitamins A, D, E and K. Try to avoid trans fats or saturated fats. Look always for foods with monounsaturated fats and polyunsaturated fats.

Fiber- Fiber slows sugar absorption into the bloodstream, it also helps your body absorb nutrients from some foods. Lastly Fiber may reduce your appetite making you feel full and satisfied.

MINERALS

	FUNCTIONS	SOURCES
CALCIUM	Strengthens bones, teeth, muscle function.	Milk, broccoli, whey, yogurt, dark green vegetables, legumes.
PHOSPHORUS	Regulates blood cells, stronger bones and teeth.	Meat, poultry, fish, nuts.
MAGNESIUM	Nerve and muscle function, temperature control, bone growth, converts blood sugar into energy.	Soybeans, corn, grains, avocado, leafy greens.
MANGANESE	Nerve function, blood and bone formation.	Spinach, almonds, sweet potato, green tea.
ZINC	Growth skin, aids in digestion, brain and muscles, fertility, antioxidant.	Red meat, eggs, seafood.
COOPER	Aids in formation of red blood cells, skin protein, nerves and joints.	Almonds, sunflower seeds, avocado, broccoli, garlic, orange, raisin.
SELENIUM	Works with vitamin E to promote antibodies, protects body tissue.	Seafood, meat, grains.
POTASSIUM	Fluid balance, muscle function, lower blood pressure, production and translocation of carbohydrates.	Avocados, banana, potato, spinach, fish, beans, citrus fruits.
IRON	Improves blood cells quality, healthy immune system, carries oxygen to the tissues.	Beef, poultry, eggs, shellfish, dried fruits.